# Implementing the Common Core State Standards through Mathematical Problem Solving

## Grades 6–8

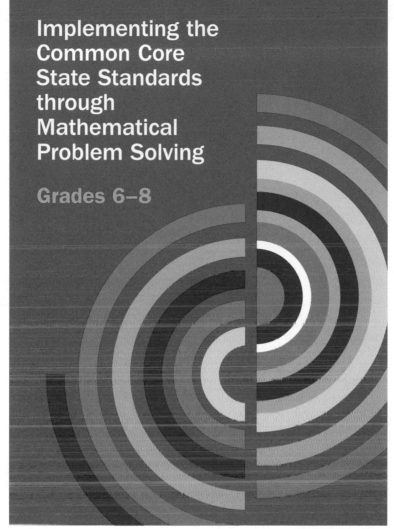

Theresa J. Gurl
Alice F. Artzt
Alan Sultan
*Queens College of the City University of New York*

Frances R. Curcio, Series Editor
*Queens College of the City University of New York*

NATIONAL COUNCIL OF
TEACHERS OF MATHEMATICS

Copyright © 2013 by
The National Council of Teachers of Mathematics, Inc.
1906 Association Drive, Reston, VA 20191-1502
(703) 620-9840; (800) 235-7566; www.nctm.org
All rights reserved
Second printing 2014

Library of Congress Cataloging-in-Publication Data

Gurl, Theresa J.

  Implementing the common core state standards through mathematical problem solving. Grades 6–8 / Theresa J. Gurl, Alice F. Artzt, and Alan Sultan, Queens College of the City University of New York ; Frances R. Curcio, series editor, Queens College of the City University of New York.

  pages cm

Includes bibliographical references.

ISBN 978-0-87353-709-4

1.  Problem solving—Study and teaching (Middle school)—Standards—United States.
2.  Mathematics—Study and teaching (Middle school)—Standards—United States.  I. Artzt, Alice F. II. Sultan, Alan. III. Title.

QA63.G869 2013

510.71'273—dc23

2013013223

The National Council of Teachers of Mathematics is the public voice of mathematics education, supporting teachers to ensure equitable mathematics learning of the highest quality for all students through vision, leadership, professional development, and research.

Printed in the United States of America

# Contents

# Series Editor's Foreword

The purpose of *Implementing the Common Core State Standards through Mathematical Problem Solving: Grades 6–8,* as well as that of the other books in the series (those for kindergarten–grade 2, grades 3–5, and high school), is to (1) provide examples of how instruction that focuses on developing mathematical problem-solving skills supports the Common Core State Standards (CCSS), (2) help teachers interpret the standards in ways that are useful for practice, and (3) provide examples of rich mathematical tasks and ways of implementing them in the classroom that have specific links to multiple standards. The books in this series are not meant to be comprehensive collections of mathematics problems for the entire school curriculum; instead, they contain rich problems and tasks on selected topics designed to develop several mathematics concepts presented in ways that illustrate the connections and interrelatedness between the CCSS and mathematical problem solving.

## The Common Core State Standards for Mathematics

In June 2010, responding to the declining achievement of United States schoolchildren in reading and mathematics both nationally and internationally, the National Governors' Association and the Council for Chief State School Officers (NGA Center and CCSSO) issued the *Common Core State Standards* (http://www.corestandards.org). The CCSS program is a unified, national effort to strengthen the ability of future citizens to be globally competitive, while preparing them for college and career readiness. The standards and practices across the grades are expectations for improving the teaching and learning of mathematics. Toward this concerted effort, a large majority of the states, along with the Washington, D.C., school system, have adopted CCSS.

Similar to the standards in *Principles and Standards for School Mathematics* (NCTM 2000), the essential content in the Common Core State Standards for Mathematics (CCSSM) for grades 6–8 is included in several content areas ("domains") with various degrees of specificity: Ratios and Proportional Relationships, the Number System, Expressions and Equations, Functions (in grade 8 only), Geometry, and Statistics and Probability. Modeling is expected to be integrated throughout the content areas. An overview of the CCSS standards for middle and high school mathematics is included in the appendix.

For each content area, the eight Standards for Mathematical Practice, which may be considered as fundamental elements of mathematical problem solving, are stated as follows:

## CCSS Standards for Mathematical Practice

**MP.1** Make sense of problems and persevere in solving them.

**MP.2** Reason abstractly and quantitatively.

**MP.3** Construct viable arguments and critique the reasoning of others.

**MP.4** Model with mathematics.

**MP.5** Use appropriate tools strategically.

**MP.6** Attend to precision.

**MP.7** Look for and make use of structure.

**MP.8** Look for and express regularity in repeated reasoning. (NGA Center and CCSSO 2010)

These practices are highlighted throughout the problem-solving tasks and activities contained in each of the books in this series.

# Mathematical Problem Solving

Although problem solving has always been a goal of mathematics instruction, Pólya's helpful guide, *How to Solve It* (1957), had been in print for several decades before the publication of *An Agenda for Action* in 1980, in which the National Council of Teachers of Mathematics (NCTM) asserted the importance of mathematical problem solving in the school curriculum. That is, *"the mathematics curriculum should be organized around problem solving"* (NCTM 1980, p. 2, original in italics).

But what is mathematical problem solving? Throughout the years, although not research-based, instruction in developing mathematical problem-solving skills has relied on Pólya's (1957) four-step approach—understanding the problem, developing a plan, carrying out the plan, and looking back to determine whether the solution makes sense.

At the heart of the problem-solving process is determining what consists of a problem for learners of mathematics. Different from a familiar exercise or example for which learners have a prescribed approach for obtaining a solution, a "problem" is usually nonroutine and nontraditional, and the learner needs to bring strategies, tools, and insights to bear in order to solve it (Henderson and Pingry 1953). In the late 1980s, textbooks and supplemental resource materials highlighted various problem-solving strategies to assist learners in approaching and solving problems. Such strategies as guessing and checking, using a drawing, making a table or an organized list, finding a pattern, using logical reasoning, solving a simpler problem, and working backward (O'Daffer 1988) became staples of mathematics instruction.

Much of the research on mathematical problem solving was conducted in the mid-1970s through the late 1980s (Schoenfeld 2007). The intent was not to focus on solving a given problem but rather on examining how to help learners develop strategies to tackle problems and real-world applications. Throughout the years, as attempts have been made to manage the complexity of studying various aspects of mathematical problem solving, research attention has been redirected to mathematical modeling (Lesh and Zawojewski 2007; Lester and Kehle 2003). According to Henry Pollak:

> Problem solving may not refer to the outside world at all. Even when it does, problem solving usually begins with the idealized real-world situation in mathematical terms, and ends with a mathematical result. Mathematical modeling, on the other hand, begins in the "unedited" real world, requires problem formulating before problem solving, and once the problem is solved, moves back into the real world where the results are considered in their original context. (Pollak 2011)

The Common Core State Standards suggest that instruction in mathematics integrate modeling in mathematical tasks and activities, and they identify specific standards for which modeling is recommended, thus challenging teachers, curriculum developers, and textbook authors to bring authentic, real-world data into the classroom. Through mathematical problem solving and modeling, students' experience in mathematics will extend beyond traditional, routine word problems.

With its Essential Understanding (NCTM 2010–13) and Reasoning and Sense Making (NCTM 2009–10) series, NCTM has offered ideas to help teachers actively involve students in analyzing and solving problems. This newer series, Implementing the Common Core through Mathematical Problem Solving, contributes to these efforts, specifically supporting the connections between CCSS and mathematical problem solving.

The authors of this book, Theresa Gurl, Alice Artzt, and Alan Sultan, are gratefully acknowledged for sharing their insights and ideas to help mathematics teachers of grades 6–8 meet the challenges of implementing the Common Core. Thanks are due to the NCTM Educational Materials Committee for making the development of this manuscript possible, and to Joanne Hodges, senior director of publications, Myrna Jacobs, publications manager, and the NCTM publications staff for their guidance, advice, and technical support in the preparation of the manuscript.

**Frances R. Curcio**
*Series Editor*

# Preface

Students entering middle school are at the beginning of their academic transition from the somewhat concrete realm of elementary school mathematics to the more abstract mathematics required in preparation for high school. The middle school curriculum—with its emphasis on connecting arithmetic concepts to ratio and proportion, beginning notions of "variable" and algebra, statistical thinking, number, and geometric concepts—provides rich opportunities for students to learn and do mathematics through problem solving. Middle school students can benefit from both independent and collaborative problem-solving opportunities. As stated in *Principles and Standards for School Mathematics* (NCTM 2000): "Problem solving in grades 6–8 should promote mathematical learning. Students can learn about, and deepen their understanding of, mathematical concepts by working through carefully selected problems that allow applications of mathematics to other contexts" (NCTM 2000, p. 256).

Building on NCTM recommendations (NCTM 2011), the Common Core State Standards for Mathematics (CCSSM) further develop the standards for how students should go about doing mathematics, and thus include standards for "mathematical practice" in addition to standards for "mathematical content." Teachers have the new challenge of maintaining an environment conducive to problem solving in their classrooms while meeting the requirements of the Common Core State Standards. The purpose of this book is to provide a guide for middle school teachers in their efforts to implement these standards, both for mathematical content and for mathematical practice. As the title suggests, there is an emphasis on meeting the standards through a problem-solving approach, not only as a means of practicing what has been learned but as a tool to "build new mathematical knowledge" (NCTM 2000, p. 52). Overall, the Common Core State Standards for Mathematics are well suited for a problem-solving approach.

To develop mathematical problem-solving skills and to support the Common Core Standards, we highlight two approaches. First, rich problems are presented that provide an entry point for lessons, and not simply an opportunity to practice what has already been learned. Our hope is that teachers will use these problems to launch lessons and allow the embedded mathematics to be revealed through classroom discourse. The second approach is to present a carefully designed series of expressions and questions that allow mathematical ideas to emerge. We note that each section does not have an equal treatment of the two approaches, as certain concepts and problems lend themselves differently to each. Problems were written with the interests of middle school students in mind.

The Common Core State Standards emphasize both conceptual and procedural understanding, and attention to the underlying structure of mathematical concepts and procedures (National Governors Association Center for Best Practices [NGA Center] and Council of Chief State School Officers [CCSSO] 2010). The standards do not advocate any particular type of teaching or pedagogical approach. Implicit, however, in the Standards for Mathematical Practice (as listed on page vi) is a student-centered approach that facilitates students' ability to communicate with each other in order to create arguments and critique the arguments and reasoning of others.

This book is organized by the major CCSSM content areas for grades 6–8, with a chapter for each of four domains—Ratio and Proportion, the Number System, Geometry, and Statistics and Probability—and a fifth chapter combining the domain of Expressions and Equations with that of Functions. Each chapter includes several problems (labeled "tasks") for each domain, with each task targeting specific clusters of standards. The book has thirty-seven tasks in all. Although every domain required of all students is represented, not every individual standard or cluster is incorporated. Interesting problems that lend themselves to meaningful implementation of content standards have been included. Our intent was not to be exhaustive, but to present exemplary problems as models for teachers. At the end of each section, the Standards for Mathematical Practice best met by the problems in the section are discussed. Although the temptation for busy teachers may be to only look at the tasks themselves, we hope that teachers also read the discussion of the problems. The discussion sections provide ideas for implementing the tasks, possibly modifying them, and avoiding common misconceptions related to the concepts inherent in the tasks. In many cases, the modifications make suggestions about how to implement the problem on a different grade level.

This book is intended for use by middle school mathematics teachers looking for support in implementing the CCSSM. It may be used to enhance a traditional text for students, providing a source for rich problems to motivate and launch lessons as well as to exemplify mathematics learning through problem solving. In many cases, suggestions for modifying or extending the problems are given so that instruction may be differentiated. Teacher educators may use this book as a supplemental text in a methods or curriculum course for preservice teachers in middle school mathematics. This would help preservice teachers become familiar with the Common Core State Standards for Mathematics and how they may be implemented. Finally, teachers should find the CCSS Overview for Middle and High School Mathematics, found in the appendix, helpful in providing a "vertical" overview of the major content areas and how they are emphasized through the middle and high school grades.

## Chapter 1

# Ratios and Proportional Relationships

The concepts of ratio and proportional reasoning are "big ideas" that permeate the middle school curriculum. The Common Core State Standards for Mathematics (CCSSM) consider these topics as one of five critical areas of the curriculum in both grade 6 and grade 7.

A ratio is a type of numerical comparison. Prior to middle school, students have been making *absolute* comparisons, using additive notions, to determine whether one quantity is more than, less than, or equal to, another. *Relative* comparisons, using multiplicative notions, allow quantities to be compared in a different way. For example, consider two different groups of students, each including both girls and boys. The first group has 20 girls, while the second group has 25. Clearly, the second group has more girls, using an absolute comparison. If we learn, however, that the first group has a total of 30 students while the second has a total of 150 students, we can make different types of comparisons for the number of girls, both to the total number of students in each group and to the number of boys in each group. Using a relative comparison, we see that the first group (20 girls out of 30 students) has more girls relative to the total number of students in it than the second (25 girls out of 150 students). If we consider a third group with 40 girls out of a total of 60 students, we see that the relative number of girls in the first group and the third is the same. The notions of *ratio* and *equal ratio* (or *proportion*) emerge naturally from such scenarios.

The type of thinking exemplified above is the conceptual underpinning for the big ideas of ratio and proportion, which are that ratio is a multiplicative comparison, and that proportional situations are based on multiplicative, and not additive, relationships (Van de Walle 1998). These notions are related to various ways of thinking about proportional concepts and their representations, including unit rate, equations and functions, graphing, and percent. As stated in *Principles and Standards for School Mathematics*, proportionality connects many of the mathematics topics studied in grades 6–8.

> Facility with proportionality involves much more than setting two ratios equal and solving for a missing term. It involves recognizing quantities that are related proportionally and using numbers, tables, graphs and equations to think about the quantities and their relationship. (NCTM 2000, p. 217)

It is essential to give students opportunities to develop a conceptual understanding of proportion so that solving problems involving proportion is not reduced to the procedure of cross multiplication only. It is worth noting that the Common Core State Standards require that students solve problems using proportional reasoning, not specifically using the cross product.

1

The CCSSM middle school standards include a Ratios and Proportional Relationships domain for grades 6 and 7 (though not one for grade 8). The single overarching standard in this domain for grade 6 is "Understand ratio concepts and use ratio reasoning to solve problems" (National Governors Association Center for Best Practices [NGA Center] and Council of Chief State School Officers [CCSSO] 2010, p. 42). These concepts include setting up ratios to represent real-life situations, unit rates, and using various representations to solve problems, including tables, graphs, and equations; percent concepts are also included in grade 6. The one overarching standard in the ratio and proportion domain for grade 7 is "Analyze proportional relationships and use them to solve real-world and mathematical problems" (NGA Center and CCSSO 2010, p. 48). In grade 7, students compute unit rates in more complex situations and examine proportional relationships in various situations, including the constant of proportionality and equations. More complex ratio and percent problems are also part of the CCSSM standards for grade 7.

Although ratio and proportion are not topics with separate domains in the standards for grade 8 and high school, proportional reasoning is present when working with similar figures, notions of trigonometry, and probabilistic concepts. The standards for grades 6 and 7 are structured so that students are ready for these more difficult concepts in grade 8 and high school.

What follows are six tasks to support ratio reasoning (tasks 1.1 and 1.2), percent (tasks 1.3 and 1.4), and proportion (tasks 1.5 and 1.6). The eight Standards for Mathematical Practice (MP), as listed on page vi, are woven throughout these domains. Depending on the problem, a subset of those standards is discussed. The problems are loosely grouped by grade level, although the extensions of some problems might allow students to meet a higher grade's standards. As in other chapters, we believe that all of these problems require "attention to precision," thus developing mathematically proficient students as required by the sixth Standard for Mathematical Practice. The tasks in this chapter are summarized in table 1.1.

Table 1.1

*Content areas, grade levels, and standards met by the tasks in chapter 1*

| Content Areas | Tasks | Grade 6 Standards | Grade 7 Standards | Grade 8 Standards | Standards for Mathematical Practice |
|---|---|---|---|---|---|
| Ratio reasoning | 1.1 | 6.RP.1, 6.RP.3 | | 8.F.4* | MP.1, MP.2 |
| Ratio reasoning | 1.2 | 6.RP.1 | | | MP.1, MP.2 |
| Percent | 1.3 | | 7.RP.3 | 8.F.4* | MP.3, MP.4 |
| Percent | 1.4 | | 7.RP.3 | | MP.3, MP.4 |
| Proportion | 1.5 | 6.RP.2, 6.RP.3a | 7.RP.2a, 2b, 2c, 2d | 8.F.2, 8.F.4* | MP.1, MP.4 |
| Proportion | 1.6 | | 7.RP.1, 7.RP.2, 7.RP.3 | | MP.1, MP.4 |

*Extensions of the problem

# Ratio Concepts

## Grade 6

The first task in this section begins to lay the groundwork for ratio concepts and proportional thinking by giving students the opportunity to see the need for relative comparisons and how they are different from absolute (or additive) comparisons. Task 1.1 lends itself well to a problem-solving approach. Students need to understand the problem, and particularly what is different about its parts (*a*) and (*b*), in order to make sense of what is being asked in later parts of the problem, and to be able to devise a plan to approach the problem. In devising such a plan, students might, for example, draw a picture to visually compare the number of goals made and attempted in each part of the problem.

This task addresses the standard 6.RP.1, "Understand the concept of a ratio and use ratio language to describe a ratio relationship between two quantities," and 6.RP.3, "Use ratio and rate reasoning to solve real-world and mathematical problems" (NGA Center and CCSSO 2010, p. 42).

## Task 1.1

Anna and Gerard both play basketball. In a recent game, Anna took 10 shots at the basket and made 3 of them, while Gerard took 20 shots and made 5 of them. (In this context, "making" a shot means the ball goes into the basket.)

- (*a*) Who made more baskets in this game?
- (*b*) Who performed better in this game?
- (*c*) What is different about questions (*a*) and (*b*)? Why is "performing better" different from making more baskets? What arithmetic operations did you use to answer questions (*a*) and (*b*)?
- (*d*) In a later game, Anna attempted 14 shots and Gerard attempted 20. Write your own two scenarios using those numbers:
  - One in which Anna and Gerard made different numbers of baskets, but performed equally well
  - One in which Anna made fewer baskets than Gerard, but Anna performed better

Parts (*a*) and (*b*) of task 1.1 each ask students a question that, on a first reading, might be misinterpreted to mean the same thing. The goal of these questions is to juxtapose the idea of absolute and relative comparison so that students can make a distinction between them. Teachers should introduce the language of ratio as a type of comparison when discussing this problem. In the second scenario of part (*d*), the idea of equal ratios is introduced.

Several changes and extensions may be made to this problem. Certainly, different contexts may be used. Continuing with the sports theme, students may consider turns at bat in baseball or the number of shots in a hockey game. The discussion of the number of boys and girls in a classroom may be used (as in the introduction earlier in this chapter). Teachers may consider different contexts as appropriate given the interests of their students. Students may find the idea of a test more obvious, since it might be easier to see that answering more questions correctly does not necessarily mean that one's test score will be higher if the number of questions is different.

Extensions to the mathematical aspects of the problem may be made as well. Students may be asked to find the percent of shots made in parts (*b*) and (*d*). Students may also be asked to answer further questions involving proportional reasoning. For example, the following question could be asked in part (*d*): *Michael attempted 12 shots but performed equally well as Anna and Gerard. How many baskets did he make?* A more open-ended extension to the same part of the problem might ask the following: *Michael performed as well as Anna and Gerard. Write two different possibilities for the number of shots he attempted and made.* Alternatively, the question could ask for a possibility of the number of shots attempted and made if he performed worse or better. In order to bring percent, as in standard 6.RP.3c (NGA Center and CCSSO 2010, p. 42) into this problem, students could be asked to find the percent of baskets made for each of the players. Finally, students could be given a particular unit rate for "shots made" as compared to attempted, and be asked to make tables of equivalent ratios. Students might be asked to plot points representing the equivalent ratios, considering one of the values as a function of the other, thus making this problem meet the grade 8 standard 8.F.4, "Construct a function to model a linear relationship between two quantities" (NGA Center and CCSSO 2010, p. 55). Predictions could then be made, such as "If Anna attempted 40 shots, predict how many she made," or other similar questions.

The next activity gives students the opportunity to formalize their use of the ideas and language of ratio. Although the task is conceptually simpler than task 1.1, the two tasks are ordered this way because task 1.1 creates a need for relative comparison first, while task 1.2 gives students the opportunity to respond to an open-ended question about ratio. This allows for informal conceptual development first, followed by formalization using proper mathematical language. This problem is open-ended and gives students the opportunity to practice writing their own ratios given a scenario involving books. The suggested extensions of the problem allow for a deeper discussion of the meaning of "smaller" and "larger" ratios. Task 1.2 is targeted for students to meet standard 6.RP.1, "Understand the concept of a ratio and use ratio language to describe a ratio relationship between two quantities" (NGA Center and CCSSO 2010, p. 42).

## Task 1.2

Tariq has several types of items on his J-Pad. He has 30 applications ("apps"), some songs, and 18 books. The books include 10 mysteries and 8 books focused on sports. He is not sure how many songs there are on the device.

(*a*) What is the ratio of the number of apps to the number of books?

(*b*) What is the ratio of the number of books to the number of apps?

(*c*) Write some other ratios that compare the number of items of one type to the number of items of another type in words and in symbols.

(*d*) Tariq realizes that the ratio of the number of mysteries to the number of apps is the same as the ratio of the number of books to the number of songs. How many songs must he have?

Students might be resistant to writing ratios involving the number of songs in part (*c*) because they need to use a variable to represent this number. They should, however, be encouraged to write ratios using variables. Therefore, teachers may want to require in part (*c*) that at least one ratio they write include the number of songs. This problem helps students develop flexibility in their thinking, as they need to make the decision about which comparisons to make and the order in which to make them.

The four parts of the task could be extended in a variety of ways. One possible extension of this problem would be to ask what percent of the total number of items is of a particular type. Students would need to have a specific value for the number of songs in order to do this, so this might be done following part (*d*).

Part (*d*) as written only has one answer, but teachers may also extend this part of the problem by introducing the concept of "larger" or "smaller" ratios. This not only makes the question open-ended, but it also introduces the difficult notion of comparing ratios that are not necessarily equal. A possible modification of part (*d*) is "Tariq knows that the ratio of the number of mysteries to the number of apps is smaller than the ratio of the number of books to the number of songs. What is a possible number of songs that he has?" Students must then realize that the ratio of the number of mysteries to the number of apps is $^{10}/_{30}$, or equivalently $^1/_3$, and determine a number of songs so that the ratio $18/s$ (where $s$ is the number of songs) is less than $^1/_3$. Any value of $s$ that is greater than 54 will meet the requirement. Students may also be asked what the smallest value for $s$ would be that would meet the requirement. It may seem counterintuitive that having a larger number of books makes the ratio smaller, but this is a good opportunity to remind students about the relationships among fractions. Further, students should see that only integral values for $s$ make sense for this problem.

Similarly, the questions may be modified by saying that the ratio of the number of mysteries to apps is larger than the ratio of books to songs. In this case the ratio $18/s$ would need to be greater than $^1/_3$, so any integral value for $h$ that is less than 54 and greater than zero would be a solution. It would also be worthwhile for teachers to ask students why zero could not be a value for $s$.

## DISCUSSION—*Tasks 1.1 and 1.2*

Tasks 1.1 and 1.2 require the use of various problem-solving strategies, thus allowing students to meet several of the CCSSM standards through the approach of making sure they understand what is being asked in the problem, making a plan for how to solve it, apply-ing a strategy, and checking whether their answer makes sense. An appropriate strategy for task 1.1 might be to "draw a picture" or "use a model." Students may need to repre-sent the comparison of shots made to shots attempted by visually representing the values, either on a number line or graph paper, or by using a discrete or concrete representation, such as dots or circles, or centimeter cubes, to represent the quantities. Such scale rep-resentations may help students more clearly see the meaning of relative comparison. An additional strategy that might be successful for task 1.2 would be to "use direct reason-ing," working directly from the given information. Students may also benefit from using a model for this problem, such as drawing a picture or making a model using concrete or semi-concrete materials. For part (*d*) of task 1.2 and its extension, a productive approach might be "guess and check" or "work backwards," choosing values that make the ratio smaller (or larger) and determining how this fits the problem. For both problems, stu-dents should check their work and determine whether their solutions make sense. For example, if students write an inequality, such as $x > 54$, for their solution to the extension of the problem that asks for a smaller ratio, they need to examine whether non-integral values make sense in this problem and adjust the representation of their answer. Several of the CCSSM Standards for Mathematical Practice are targeted by these problems.

## MP.1

Tasks 1.1 and 1.2 both require that students "make sense of problems and persevere in solving them" (NGA Center and CCSSO 2010, p. 6). Parts (*a*) and (*b*) of task 1.1 juxtapose two types of comparison, absolute and relative, that may not initially make sense to stu-dents. Students must think through and understand what the problem is asking them to do. In task 1.2, students must decide how to represent the unknown value of books using a variable, and then determine how to create equal, larger, or smaller ratios by examining different values of the variable.

## MP.2

In developing the ideas of proportional reasoning through each of the above tasks, students "reason abstractly and quantitatively" (NGA Center and CCSSO 2010, p. 6). Students must make sense of the different types of reasoning used when making abso-lute comparisons, simply saying that one quantity is more (or less) than another, and making relative comparisons, saying that one quantity is more (or less) *relative* to another. Further, the extension of task 1.2 requires that students compare the actual ratios, determining what it means for a ratio to be smaller or larger than another ratio.

# Percent

## Grade 7

The tasks that follow target misconceptions that students often have about percent. Students often erroneously try to "operate" on percent values as though they were absolute quantities, and they forget that the percent is a relative quantity. Task 1.3 presents students with a context that allows them to consider whether this makes sense. Although it might seem reasonable to students initially, once they see that they eventually obtain a percent greater than 100 they should conclude that something is "wrong" and revisit their approach to the problem. Students should be given part (*a*) first, then after some thought and discussion they can be given part (*b*).

## Task 1.3

Bright-O toothpaste advertises that 30 percent of tooth stains are removed after 1 week of use. As Gabriella was brushing her teeth, she thought, "Well, if I use this toothpaste for 2 weeks, then 60 percent of the stains will be gone, and if I use it for 3 weeks, then 90 percent of the stains will be gone."

   (*a*)  According to Gabriella's reasoning, what percent of stains will be gone after 4 weeks? Does this make sense? Why or why not?

   (*b*)  Now that you have seen the flaw in Gabriella's reasoning, what is a reasonable way to compute the percent of stains that have been removed after 2 weeks? 3 weeks? 5 weeks?

Although this type of problem might seem quite sophisticated for students in the middle grades, the concepts targeted are critical to students' understanding of percent. Of course, according to Gabriella's reasoning, 120 percent of the stains will be removed after 4 weeks, which is not sensible, and indicates fundamental misconceptions about percent. Teachers might first want to discuss with students what an advertiser might even mean by assigning a percent to such a statement, and how "stains" might be quantified and measured. As an aside, teachers might have a short discussion about misleading advertisements.

   To initiate a discussion of the problem, teachers may want to assign a value to quantify the beginning "measure" of stains—say, 100. Of course, any value may be used, but using 100 helps illuminate the fact that if 30 percent of the stains are removed, then 70 percent remain. If we consider the number of stains remaining after one week, we can see that if we begin with 100, we subtract 30 percent of 100, that is $100 - 0.3(100) = 70$. At the start of the second week, the beginning value has changed, and is now 70. So, after two weeks, we subtract 30 percent of 70 from 70. That is, 70 − 0.3(70) = 49. The same reasoning follows: At the beginning of the third week we begin with 49, and the logic continues. Students may notice that if they must subtract what is being removed, it makes more sense to consider what remains. They may also notice that the value at the end of the first week is 0.7(100), at the end of the second week is 0.7 • 0.7(100), and at the end of the third week is 0.7 • 0.7 • 0.7(100), leading to the use of exponents.

The observation that we can work with the stains that remain can give students the opportunity to work with functions. This might be a bit sophisticated for most seventh graders, but can lend itself to informal work with exponential functions of the form $y = ab^x$, where $a$ is the initial value, $b = 0.7$, and $x$ is the number of weeks that the toothpaste has been used.

Other extensions of this problem would be to ask such questions as "How many weeks does it take to remove at least 75 percent of the stains?" The given problem may also be changed so that, instead of the advertisement stating that 30 percent of stains are removed, different rates of removal are used for different effects.

The next task also targets misconceptions about percent. Students do not always make the connection that for percents to be equal, they must be percents of the same quantity. The context of task 1.4, a sale at a store, is one with which many students are familiar. The scenario, with a "percent-off" sale, then an additional percent off of the sale price, is common in many stores.

## Task 1.4

Kara is shopping at her favorite store, which is holding a sale that offers 20 percent off the price of every item in the store. She has a coupon that gives her an additional 50 percent off the sale price. She thinks this is great, because now she will get 70 percent off on the items she buys.

(*a*) Is Kara correct? Explain.

(*b*) If Kara wants to buy an item that originally costs $60, how much will the item cost given both discounts?

(*c*) If the tax rate is 7.5 percent, what will be the final cost of the item in part (*b*)?

(*d*) Which is the better deal: 20 percent off with an additional 50 percent off the sale price, or 50 percent off with an additional 20 percent off the sale price?

Part (*a*) targets a common misconception, which is that the percents can simply be added. Of course, this is not the case since the second percent is taken off of a smaller number. Teachers may decide to have students compute the sale price by first subtracting 20 percent of the original cost, then subtracting 50 percent of the sale price to determine final cost, and comparing this answer to subtracting 70 percent of the cost. Students will see that this is not the same result. Class discussion can help clarify that the discount is smaller because the percent is taken off of the sale price, which is lower than the original cost. This problem also opens up the opportunity to discuss the rather perplexing convention of computing a "percent off" and subtracting it from the original cost, instead of the simpler idea of computing what percent will be paid. That is, for an item whose cost is represented by $C$, it makes more sense to determine the cost at 20 percent off by considering that 80 percent of the price will be paid, and multiplying $0.8 \cdot C$, rather than by computing $C - 0.2 \cdot C$. Teachers may wish to discuss this with their students.

Part (*d*) brings up the interesting question of order, and students may be surprised to see that the order in which the discounts are taken does not matter. If the cost of an item is represented by $C$, we see that what we pay, which equals $C \cdot 0.8 \cdot 0.5$, is the same as $C \cdot 0.5 \cdot 0.8$ due to the commutativity of multiplication of real numbers. Further, when computing tax along with a discount, it does not matter whether the tax is computed first, then the discount taken (as long as the discount is also taken on the tax) or whether the discount is taken first, then the tax computed (as long as the tax is only computed on the discounted amount).

Finally, this task sets the stage for asking the somewhat bigger and more general question "Which is a bigger discount, 80 percent or 10 percent?" Of course, many students instinctively might answer that 80 percent is bigger, but the more important question is "Of what?" If the percents are of the same amount, then 80 percent of it is certainly bigger, but 80 percent of 5 is not bigger than 10 percent of 1000. This reconnects to the idea of relative comparison as opposed to absolute comparison as discussed earlier in this chapter.

## DISCUSSION—*Tasks 1.3 and 1.4*

Employing problem-solving strategies will aid in students' success in solving the problems presented in tasks 1.3 and 1.4. In understanding what is being asked in each of the problems, students must understand that problems involving percent do not make sense until the answer to the question "Of what?" is determined. Students might make a chart or organize a list to answer each of the questions. When checking their answers, students need to determine whether their answers make sense in the context of the original problem.

**MP.3**

Tasks 1.3 and 1.4 both present students with the opportunity to examine and critique the approach of a fictional student, and to determine that the approach is flawed in some way. Students must then determine what the correct approach to each of the problems is and explain their answers, thus "construct[ing] viable arguments and critiqu[ing] the reasoning of others" (NGA Center and CCSSO 2010, p. 6). Specifically, task 1.3 asks students to determine the flaw in Gabriella's thinking when she multiplies a percent by an integer, not realizing that the percent is of a different amount. Task 1.4 asks students to consider that percents cannot simply be added when they are percents of different amounts.

**MP.4**

The real-life situations presented in tasks 1.3 and 1.4 require that students "model with mathematics"; specifically, they must "identify important quantities in a practical situation" and "interpret their mathematical results in the context of the situation and reflect on whether the results make sense" (NGA Center and CCSSO 2010, p. 7). Task 1.3 presents students with an advertising context that they are likely to see in their everyday life, but do not usually have the opportunity to analyze mathematically. Similarly, task 1.4 gives students the opportunity to analyze a situation involving a sale with which they might be familiar.

# Proportion

## Grades 6 and 7

Tasks 1.5 and 1.6 present students with real-life contexts in which they must use proportional reasoning to solve problems. The tasks synthesize several ideas, including percent, making tables, and plotting points, as well as examining unit rate and slope in the context of functions, if teachers wish to integrate functions into this topic. Task 1.5 gives students a price for 60 chocolate candies and a different monetary contribution from five different students, and it asks students to divide the chocolate in proportion to the amount paid by each student. In part (*a*) of the task, students are asked to determine how many chocolates each person should get in an unstructured way. Students may be encouraged to brainstorm in pairs, and they may decide to determine the unit rate per chocolate, or to make a table to compare the different values.

Later parts of the problem provide more structure for different approaches, and because of this, teachers might want to give part (*a*) first, and then, after eliciting different approaches, have students do the later parts of the problem. Task 1.5 addresses the grade 6 standards 6.RP.2, "Understand the concept of a unit rate," and 6.RP.3a, "Make tables of equivalent ratios relating quantities with whole-number measurements" (NGA Center and CCSSO 2010, p. 42). Grade 7 standard 7.RP.2, "Recognize and represent proportional relationships between quantities" (NGA Center and CCSSO 2010, p. 48), is also met.

## Task 1.5

Five friends contribute money to buy 60 chocolate candies. In total, the chocolate candies cost $15. The friends contribute as follows, and they want to divide the chocolate candies fairly, based on what was paid:

| Carmen | $3 |
|--------|-----|
| Luwen  | $1 |
| Julia  | $4 |
| Otis   | $5 |
| Quinn  | $2 |

(*a*) How many chocolate candies should each friend get, based on what was paid? Explain how you approached this problem.

(*b*) Make a table that compares the amount paid by each friend to the number of chocolate candies they should receive. Plot the values in your table on a coordinate plane. What do you notice about all of the points you plotted?

(*c*) What is the unit rate for the cost of chocolate candies?

(*d*) A different friend, Rachel, went to a different store, and purchased 10 chocolate candies for $2. Plot the coordinates associated with these values on the same graph as part (*b*). What do you notice about the point you just plotted in relation to the line? What is different about the price Rachel paid?

Teachers may elect to take several different approaches with students to this problem. The intention of the problem as written is to give students part (*a*) first, allowing them to think about it alone, and then brainstorm in pairs, or as a whole class. If students get stuck, the teacher might ask such questions as, "What fraction of the total payment was made by Carmen?" and "What fraction of the chocolate candies should Carmen get?" Students might decide to make a table or to determine the unit rate for the cost of chocolate candies.

Part (*b*) asks students to make a table (they might have already done this) and to plot the points on the coordinate plane. The problem does not, however, tell students which variable should be dependent and which independent. Therefore, students may end up with a line whose slope is 4, and the unit rate is "four chocolate candies for one dollar" or a line whose slope is $1/4$, and the unit rate is "one chocolate costs $1/4$ dollar." This idea is worth discussing with students. Students can also be asked to examine the point whose *x*-coordinate is 1, and to connect its *y*-coordinate to the unit rate. Teachers may explicitly connect slope to the unit rate to make a more direct connection to functions.

Part (*d*) requires that students plot a point with a different unit rate. Students should notice that the point does not lie on the line that they graphed in part (*b*), and teachers may ask questions to help students conclude that the unit rate for the chocolate candies in part (*d*) is different, helping them to see that different unit rates lead to different lines. As a further extension, teachers may ask students to construct a table of values based on the unit rate in part (*d*) and have them examine the different slopes and their meanings in context. Teachers may also have students write equations for either or both of the unit prices of chocolate candies.

Task 1.6 includes many of the same concepts as task 1.5, but it uses fractions, rendering the problem a bit more difficult. The problem has several parts, targeting different standards, so teachers may elect to parse out the parts of the problem over several days. This problem meets many of the same standards as task 1.5, with the addition of 7.RP.1, "Compute unit rates associated with ratios of fractions," and 7.RP.3, "Use proportional relationships to solve multistep ratio and percent problems" (NGA Center and CCSSO 2010, p. 48).

## Task 1.6

A cupcake recipe with the following ingredients yields 24 cupcakes:

$4\frac{1}{2}$ cups flour
$\frac{3}{4}$ cup sugar
1 tablespoon baking soda
2 eggs

(*a*) Owen only needs 12 cupcakes. How much of each ingredient will he need?

(*b*) To cut down on sugar, Owen's mother prefers that he only use recipes in which the volume of sugar is not more than 25 percent of the dry ingredients (not including baking soda, since the amount is so small). Would Owen's mother find this recipe acceptable?

(*c*) Use the table to determine several different equivalent ratios of flour to sugar:

| Flour | $4\frac{1}{2}$ | | | | | |
|-------|----------------|--|--|--|--|--|
| Sugar | $\frac{3}{4}$ | | | | | |

(*d*) Plot the points in part (*c*) on the coordinate plane.

(*e*) What is the ratio of flour to sugar in lowest terms? Call this value *r*.

(*f*) Plot the point (1, *r*) using the value for *r* you determined in part (*e*). What do you notice about this point in relation to the other points from part (*c*)?

(*g*) Write an equation for the proportional relationship between flour and sugar in this recipe. Use *F* to represent the number of cups of flour, and *S* to represent the number of cups of sugar.

(*h*) Eileen has a different cupcake recipe that calls for $\frac{1}{2}$ cup sugar and $2\frac{1}{2}$ cups of flour. She says that this recipe has a smaller ratio of sugar in relation to flour, and it is less sweet. Is Eileen correct?

The main point of this problem is to have students examine proportions that involve fractions, and to determine whether or not the ratio of sugar to flour is more or less than $\frac{1}{4}$, or 25 percent. The constant of proportionality can be interpreted to be 6 or $1/6$, depending on which variable students decide to plot on the horizontal and vertical axes. Part (*h*) asks students to compare ratios to determine which is smaller. Teachers may choose to extend this problem by asking students to create a table for Eileen's recipe and to graph the coordinate pairs on the same set of axes as the graph made in part (*d*).

### DISCUSSION—*Tasks 1.5 and 1.6*

Several different problem-solving approaches are appropriate for solving the problems in tasks 1.5 and 1.6. Students may wish to use several methods when devising their plan to solve each problem. In part (*a*) of task 1.5, the question is intentionally nonprescriptive, so students may decide to make a table of values or find a unit rate, or examine different representations of the ratio in order to determine their solution. When working on task 1.6, students might revert to an easier problem (perhaps one not involving fractions) so that they can better understand and solve the problem. Of course, students must check their solutions in the context of the original problem so that they can determine whether or not their answers are reasonable.

**MP.1**

When approaching tasks 1.5 and 1.6, students must make sense of each of the problems and the constraints and relationships in the given information. In task 1.5, they must be able to determine what it means to have a ratio of chocolate candies that is equal to the ratio of money they spent. In task 1.6, they must understand what it means to have a ratio of ingredients smaller than 25 percent. In both problems, students must use different analyses to determine the answers to a variety of questions about the quantities in the recipe.

**MP.4**

The realistic contexts in each of the tasks require that students model with mathematics. In both cases they are making tables and examining a variety of ways of representing the important quantities with which they are presented. They also bring in additional constraints and examine the meaning of the graph, table, and, if necessary, slope in the context of the problems.

# Chapter 2

# The Number System

A large part of the number and quantity standards for middle school in the Common Core State Standards for Mathematics (CCSSM) is that students extend and build upon the number concepts that they have been developing during the upper elementary grades. In middle school, students perform more difficult operations with fractions, including division of a fraction by a nonzero fraction. Students also develop understanding of and facility with the rational number system and work with common factors and multiples.

The birth of integers, rational numbers, and eventually irrational numbers occurred as humans needed to represent quantities that could not be represented by the counting numbers. When it was necessary to represent "nothing," zero was born, and a need to represent "quantities owed" led to the development of the negative numbers. When whole quantities were required to be divided into parts, the rational numbers were developed. An examination of the relationship among the sides of right triangles (known, of course, as the Pythagorean theorem) led to the realization that the length of the diagonal of a square whose side length was 1 unit is irrational, and thus the irrational numbers were developed.

Number concepts and operations are one of the "big ideas" that permeate the middle school curriculum. The CCSSM considers these topics one of the critical areas of the curriculum for grades 6 through 8, with a particularly strong focus in grade 6. The Number System domain for grade 6 has three clusters of standards: "apply and extend previous understandings of multiplication and division to divide fractions by fractions," "Compute fluently with multidigit numbers and find common factors and multiples," and "apply and extend previous understandings of numbers to the system of rational numbers" (National Governors Association Center for Best Practices [NGA Center] and Council of Chief State School Officers [CCSSO] 2010, pp. 42–43). In grade 7, the single cluster requires students to "apply and extend previous understandings of operations with fractions to add, subtract, multiply, and divide rational numbers" (NGA Center and CCSSO 2010, p. 48). Students are introduced to irrational numbers in grade 8, with the single cluster of standards in this domain requiring students to "know that there are numbers that are not rational, and approximate them by rational numbers" (NGA Center and CCSSO 2010, p. 54). It should be mentioned that the CCSSM considers percent separately, as part of Ratios and Proportional Relationships (see chapter 1).

Although students should have a solid grasp of the basic concepts of fractions by middle school, they often do not. Teachers can give students an opportunity to refresh their memories by asking them to place specific groups of fractions in order from least to greatest, and to remember the reason that $1/5$, for example, is smaller than $1/4$. The teacher might then remind students that one gets less pizza if a pizza is divided equally among five friends than if it were divided equally among four. Students will remember the procedures for the operations better if they understand the underlying concepts behind fractions, and eventually the concepts behind the procedures for operations, and why they work. Students should also be asked to estimate the solutions to problems with fractions, so that they can determine whether their solutions make sense. For example, when adding $1/4$ and $1/3$, students should realize that if their solution is, say $2/7$, which is less than one-half, that they have made a mistake somewhere.

What follows are nine tasks to support dividing fractions (tasks 2.1, 2.2, and 2.3), decimals and rational numbers (tasks 2.4, 2.5, and 2.6), common factors and common multiples (tasks 2.7 and 2.8), and irrational numbers (task 2.9). The eight Standards for Mathematical Practice (MP), as listed on page vi, are woven throughout these domains. Depending on the problem, a relevant subset of the standards is discussed. The problems are loosely grouped by grade level, although the extensions of some problems might allow students to meet a higher grade's standards. As in other chapters, we believe that all of the problems require "attention to precision," thus developing mathematically proficient students as required by the sixth Standard for Mathematical Practice. Table 2.1 summarizes the specific CCSSM content areas and standards, as well as the Standards for Mathematical Practice, that are met by each task.

Table 2.1
*Content areas, grade levels, and standards met by the tasks in chapter 2*

| Content Areas | Tasks | Grade 6 Standards | Grade 7 Standards | Grade 8 Standards | Standards for Mathematical Practice |
|---|---|---|---|---|---|
| Dividing Fractions | 2.1 | 6.NS.1 | | | MP.1, MP.5, MP.7 |
| Dividing Fractions | 2.2 | 6.NS.1 | | | MP.1, MP.4, MP.5, MP.7 |
| Dividing Fractions | 2.3 | 6.NS.1 | | | MP.1, MP.4, MP.5, MP.7 |
| Decimals and Rational Numbers | 2.4 | 6.NS.3, 6.NS.5 | 7.NS.1a, 7.NS.1c | | MP.2, MP.8 |
| Decimals and Rational Numbers | 2.5 | 6.NS.3 | 7.NS.2, 7.NS.3 | | MP.2, MP.8 |
| Decimals and Rational Numbers | 2.6 | 6.NS.6a, 6.NS.6c | 7.NS.2, 7.NS.3 | | MP.2, MP.8 |
| Greatest Common Factor | 2.7 | 6.NS.4 | | | MP.4, MP.5, MP.7 |
| Least Common Multiple | 2.8 | 6.NS.4 | | | MP.4, MP.5, MP.7 |
| Irrational Numbers | 2.9 | | | 8.NS.2, 8.G.8 | MP.5, MP.7 |

# Dividing Fractions

## Grade 6

The CCSSM standards for grade 6 place an emphasis on division of fractions by fractions, as stated in standard 6.NS.1, "Apply and extend previous understandings of multiplication and division to divide fractions by fractions" (NGA Center and CCSSO 2010, p. 42). This, of course, is often thought of as the algorithm "invert and multiply." This algorithm, however, is quite mysterious to students and should be developed using a conceptual foundation (Van de Walle 1998).

The following tasks provide a conceptual foundation to establish understanding of division of fractions. The first task gives students the opportunity to think about fractions in relation to a whole, without a context. The second extends the notion to a real-life context. Before embarking on task 1.1, it might be helpful to elicit from students that $1 \div 1/2$ means "how many halves fit into a whole." Be sure to emphasize that these quotients should not be computed using any algorithm, but by considering the meaning of each using concrete models or drawings. Prior to introducing the problem, teachers may also want to relate the meaning of division of integers to these problems. For example, it would be helpful to examine the meaning of $5 \div 4$, to notice that the quotient $1 1/4$ means that 4 "goes into" 5 once, with the remaining part equal to one-quarter *of the divisor*. This notion will be important for the sets of quotients in task 2.1.

## Task 2.1

Determine the quotient in each of the following sets. Write down any patterns you notice.

(a) $1 \div 1/2$, $1 \div 1/3$, $1 \div 1/4$, $1 \div 1/5$, $1 \div 1/6$

(b) $2 \div 1/2$, $2 \div 1/3$, $2 \div 1/4$, $2 \div 1/5$, $2 \div 1/6$

(c) $1 \div 1/2$, $1 \div 2/3$, $1 \div 3/4$, $1 \div 4/5$, $1 \div 5/6$

(d) $2 \div 1/2$, $2 \div 2/3$, $2 \div 3/4$, $2 \div 4/5$, $2 \div 5/6$

In part (a), students should see somewhat easily (through using drawings or models) that there are 2 halves in 1, 3 thirds in 1, and so on. Similarly, in part (b) there are 4 halves in 2, 6 thirds in 2, and so on. These problems also give students the opportunity to see that division by a fraction can result in a number larger than the dividend, which might be counterintuitive for students. Part (c) offers a set of quotients that challenge students to determine what to do with a remainder. For example, when dividing 1 by $2/3$, drawing a picture or using a concrete model can help students see that $2/3$ "goes into" 1 once, with a remainder of $1/3$. But $1/3$ is half *of the divisor*, so the quotient is $1 1/2$, or $3/2$. Similarly, when dividing 1 by $^3/_4$, $^3/_4$ "goes into" 1 once, with a remainder of $^1/_4$. But $^1/_4$ is a third *of the divisor*, so the quotient is $1^1/_3$ or $^4/_3$. Similar reasoning may be used for the other quotients in part (*c*) and part (*d*). Students should begin to see that the reciprocal of the divisor is involved with these quotients.

Task 2.2 further develops the concept of division of fractions using a real-life context. Again, students should use the contexts of the problem to answer the question so that the procedure begins to emerge naturally from the context of the problem.

## Task 2.2

In preparing for a party at their home, their mother told Mei and Liz to shop for a box of candy that would give them the lowest cost per pound. The girls decided to go their separate ways and see who could find the best buy.

(*a*) Mei found a box that cost $6.00 for a $^3/_4$-pound box of candy. How much was that per pound?

(*b*) Liz found a box that cost $5.00 for a $^2/_3$-pound box of candy. How much was that per pound?

(*c*) Who found the best buy? Explain.

(*d*) Their friend Carmen found a $^1/_2$-pound box of candy for a better buy than both Mei and Liz. What is the most Carmen could have paid for her half-pound box of candy?

(Adapted from Van de Walle 1998, p. 270)

In part (*a*), it would seem natural to determine the price of $^1/_4$ pound in order to figure out the price of a whole pound. Careful questioning and discussion can lead students to see that it would be necessary to divide $6.00 by 3 to determine the price of $^1/_4$ pound, and then multiply this by 4 to determine the cost of one pound. Similarly, in part (*b*) students should see that they need to divide the price by 2 in order to determine what $^1/_3$ pound costs, then multiply by 3 to determine the cost of one pound. Thus, the notion of multiplying by the inverse of the divisor begins to emerge. The problem ends by asking students to compare the best buy, and then asking them to determine the maximum cost for an even better buy found by Carmen. Task 2.3 provides a context for further development of the division of fractions.

## Task 2.3

Michael needs to cut strips of licorice to sell at the candy sale. He has a large piece of licorice that is $2^3/_4$ feet long. Each strip needs to be $^1/_2$ foot long, and he needs 6 strips.

(a) Does he have enough licorice to make 6 strips of the appropriate length?

(b) How many strips can he make?

(c) Is there any licorice left over? How can this length be represented?

Part (a) simply asks students to consider whether there is enough licorice to make the required number of strips of the appropriate length. Students can model this situation concretely, using strips of paper or lengths of string, or semi-concretely, using a scale drawing. Intuitively, students may see that they do not have enough licorice since they would need 3 feet in all in order to make the necessary number of strips. Parts (b) and (c) require students to respond more specifically. The models they might have made in order to answer the question in part (a) are quite useful when addressing the concepts behind the problem. For example, the model in figure 2.1 illustrates that $2^3/_4$ is equal to $^{11}/_4$.

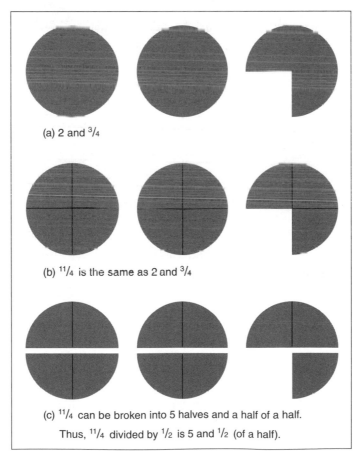

(a) 2 and $^3/_4$

(b) $^{11}/_4$ is the same as 2 and $^3/_4$

(c) $^{11}/_4$ can be broken into 5 halves and a half of a half.
Thus, $^{11}/_4$ divided by $^1/_2$ is 5 and $^1/_2$ (of a half).

Fig. 2.1. How $2^3/_4$ is equal to $^{11}/_4$, and why $^{11}/_4$ divided by $^1/_2$ is $5^1/_2$

Further, students can see that five halves "fit" into $^{11}/_4$, with some left over. Although the "leftover" part is $^1/_4$, since $^1/_4$ is half *of the divisor*, we say that the quotient is $5^1/_2$.

### DISCUSSION—*Tasks 2.1 through 2.3*

In each of tasks 2.1, 2.2, and 2.3 above, students are applying their prior knowledge about fractions to a new situation, thus generating new knowledge through problem solving. Their different approaches and various observations about what they notice when solving the problem should be organized in some way, perhaps by the teacher at the board or by using a recording sheet, so that the elements of the procedure emerge from the problems. Teachers then may formalize the procedure by eliciting ideas from the students. With this approach, students develop conceptual understanding that may help them better remember the procedure of multiplying by the reciprocal of the divisor when dividing fractions.

### MP.1

When attempting to make sense out of each of the problem situations presented in tasks 2.1, 2.2, and 2.3, students are required to "make sense of problems and persevere in solving them," and in particular, must "analyze givens, constraints, relationships, and goals" (NGA Center and CCSSO 2010, p. 6). Students must understand the meaning of each of the problems and persevere in determining each solution.

### MP.4

Tasks 2.2 and 2.3 both present problems in a real-life context for students to solve, thus students are "model[ing] with mathematics" (NGA Center and CCSSO 2010, p. 7). These problems are both practical in nature and might even be similar to problems that students have encountered in their own lives. Task 2.2 involves a situation that many people encounter when shopping, and it might even be further discussed in the context of proportional reasoning to involve the notion of a unit price. Task 2.3 involves a somewhat different context, but requires that students think about how to represent the "leftover" part.

### MP.5

If students choose to represent each of the different situations in tasks 2.1, 2,2 and 2.3 using a concrete material such as string or strips of paper, or by using a semi-concrete representation such as a drawing, they are "us[ing] appropriate tools strategically" (NGA Center and CCSSO 2010, p. 7). These tools can give the students a concrete representation of why a quantity seems to "get bigger" when divided by a fraction. (For example, 6 divided by $^1/_2$ is larger than 6 divided by 2.)

**MP.7**

When examining their various solutions for tasks 2.1 through 2.3 and examining the numbers they began with and their solutions, students must "look for and make use of structure" (NGA Center and CCSSO 2010, p. 8). Making the connection between the problem situation and the procedure for dividing fractions that emerges provides a conceptual foundation for the algorithm for dividing fractions. Task 2.2, in particular, sets the stage for students to see that if they know the price of $^3/_4$ of a pound of an item, they need to divide the price by 3 to determine the price for $^1/_4$ of a pound, then multiply by 4 to determine the price for one pound. The opportunity to see this happen repeatedly leads to the idea of multiplying by the inverse of the divisor when dividing fractions.

# Decimals and Rational Numbers

## Grades 6 and 7

The grades 6 and 7 standards for decimals and rational numbers require students to develop procedural fluency grounded in conceptual understanding that builds upon prior knowledge. Middle school students should understand that decimals are another way to represent fractions, through using place value.

The following tasks are designed to address the grade 6 standards 6.NS.3, "Fluently add, subtract, multiply, and divide multi-digit decimals using the standard algorithm for each operation"; 6.NS.5, "Understand that positive and negative numbers are used together to describe quantities having opposite directions or values"; and 6.NS.6a, "Recognize opposite signs of numbers as indicating locations on opposite sides of 0 on the number line" (NGA Center and CCSSO 2010, pp. 42–43). Although practice problems involving decimals that are closed (i.e., there is only one answer) allow students to develop computational proficiency, they can often camouflage students' underlying misconceptions. Tasks 2.4 and 2.5 give students an opportunity to use open-ended problems to develop conceptual understanding of decimals. The tasks are quite similar, but task 2.4 is related to additive concepts, while task 2.5 is related to multiplicative concepts. Part (*d*) of task 2.4 is designed to meet grade 7 standard 7.NS.1a, "Describe situations in which opposite quantities combine to make 0" (NGA Center and CCSSO 2010, p. 48), while parts (*e*) and (*f*) target standard 7.NS.1c, "Understand subtraction of rational numbers as adding the additive inverse, $p - q = p + (-q)$. Show that the distance between two rational numbers on the number line is the absolute value of their difference" (NGA Center and CCSSO 2010, p. 48). Although neither problem explicitly requires the use of a number line, teachers may elect to make number lines available to students in order to support their thinking, particularly for task 2.4.

## Task 2.4

(*a*) Two numbers written in decimal form have a sum that is less than 5. If both numbers are bigger than 2 and less than 3, what could the numbers be in decimal form?

(*b*) Two numbers written in decimal form have a sum that is equal to 5. If both numbers are bigger than 1 and less than 3, what could the numbers be in decimal form? (The numbers are not integers.)

(*c*) Two numbers written in decimal form have a sum that is equal to 2. If both numbers are bigger than zero and less than 2, what could the numbers be in decimal form if both numbers have two decimal places? (The numbers are not integers.)

(*d*) Three numbers in decimal form have a sum of zero. What could the numbers be in decimal form? (The numbers are not integers.)

(*e*) Two numbers in decimal form have a difference of 6. Both are negative. What could the numbers be in decimal form? What happens to the difference when you write the decimals in a different order? What changes about the difference? What remains the same? (The numbers are not integers.)

(*f*) Two numbers in decimal form have a difference of 6. They have opposite signs. What could the numbers be? What happens to the difference when you write the numbers in a different order? What changes about the difference? What remains the same? (The numbers are not integers.)

Of course, each part of the above task may be modified in various ways, and not all parts need to be presented to students at one time. The problems may be given with sums or differences that do not have integral values, or that have negative values, or whose differences are given to be an absolute value.

The next task relates to multiplication, and it allows students to use number sense and estimation skills to solve what might be thought of as number "puzzles." Similar to task 2.4, task 2.5 addresses standard 6.NS.3 (NGA Center and CCSSO 2010, pp. 42), as well as 7.NS.2, "Apply and extend previous understandings of multiplication and division of fractions to multiply and divide rational numbers," and 7.NS.3, "Solve real-world and mathematical problems involving the four operations with rational numbers" (NGA Center and CCSSO 2010, p. 48–49).

## Task 2.5

(*a*) 8 is multiplied by a number in decimal form. The resulting product is less than 4. What could the number be?

(b) Two numbers in decimal form have a product that is less than 6. What could the numbers in decimal form be if neither of them is a whole number?

(c) Two numbers in decimal form have a product that is less than 1. What could the numbers be?

---

Tasks 2.4 and 2.5 give students the opportunity to solve open-ended problems that can help them develop decimal number sense. There are many possibilities for modification of each of the problems. In order to require students to include signed numbers in their responses, the products given could be negative. For example, in part (*a*) the product given may be less than zero, or in parts (*b*) and (*c*) the products given may be –6 and –1, respectively. Teachers may think of other modifications that suit their students' needs.

The use of number lines can help students develop their number sense for working with rational numbers and integers. For example, plotting the products of whole numbers by fractions can remind students that multiplication does not always result in a larger number. Number lines can also help students discover the relationship of a number to its opposite, to its absolute value, and other relationships. Task 2.6 is designed to address standards for grades 6 and 7—specifically, 6.NS.6a, "Recognize opposite signs of numbers as indicating locations on opposite sides of 0 on the number line," and 6.NS.6c, "Find and position integers and other rational numbers on a horizontal or vertical number line diagram" (NGA Center and CCSSO 2012, p. 13). As with tasks 2.4 and 2.5, the grade 7 standards targeted by task 2.6 include 7.NS.2 and 7.NS.3 (NGA Center and CCSSO 2012, p. 48–49). Students may wish to use pencils of different colors for each pair of numbers in order to better see the relationships between the numbers.

---

## Task 2.6

Given points *P, Q, R, S,* and *T* on the number line, plot and label the estimate of each of the following values (see fig. 2.2). Explain your reasoning.

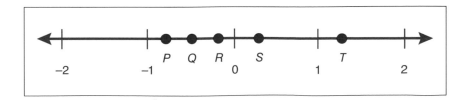

Fig. 2.2. Number line

| | | | |
|---|---|---|---|
| (*a*) abs(*S*) | (*b*) abs(*P*) | (*c*) −*S* | (*d*) −*P* |
| (*e*) *R* • *S* | (*f*) *P* • *R* | (*g*) *T* + *S* | (*h*) *T* − *S* |
| (*i*) −2 • *P* | (*j*) 2 • *P* | (*k*) *S* ÷ 1/2 | (*l*) *S* • 1/2 |

Teachers may decide to give only certain parts of the task to students to work on at a given time, and they may modify the problem to suit their needs. For example, if teachers want to work on absolute value and signed numbers with their students, they might focus on parts (*a*) through (*d*) and create additional questions similar to those. Similarly, if teachers want to work on examining the effect of multiplying numbers by fractions, they could focus on parts (*e*) and (*f*) and create additional questions similar to those two. Parts (*i*) and (*j*) allow students to compare results of multiplying by an integer with opposite signs, and parts (*k*) and (*l*) allow students to compare multiplying and dividing by a fraction. In all cases, teachers may create similar problems to what is given. Further, teachers may decide to expand (or contract) the number line given and to change the points given; for example, only using a line showing values between −1 and 1, or using a number line with a larger range of values. Task 2.6 was created as a modified version of the number line problem appearing on page 293 of NCTM's *Principles and Standards* (NCTM 2000). Teachers may wish to consult this problem for additional ideas for their students.

### DISCUSSION—*Tasks 2.4 through 2.6*

The problems given in tasks 2.4, 2.5, and 2.6 provide students with the opportunity to think about numerical problems in a conceptual way, and to carefully examine the results of different operations on the number line. In all of the above cases, teachers may decide to use the problems as a motivation for students or as a launch for their lessons. Teachers may also decide to allow their students to work cooperatively in groups or pairs to allow communication and expression of different ideas.

### MP.2

In examining each of the above numerical problems and their solutions on the number line or through careful reasoning, students are required to "reason abstractly and quantitatively" (NGA Center and CCSSO 2010, p. 6). In working with each of the values and how they change on the number line, moving to the opposite of zero or else closer to or farther from zero, students are "attending to the meaning of quantities" and "knowing and flexibly using different properties of operations and objects" (NGA Center and CCSSO 2010, p. 6). The open-ended nature of the problems in tasks 2.4 and 2.5 further requires students to reason abstractly.

**MP.8**

The repetitive nature of some of the calculations and having students examine each of the results carefully create the opportunity for students to "look for and express regularity in repeated reasoning" (NGA Center and CCSSO 2010, p. 8). If teachers together with their students compile the various responses to the problems in tasks 2.4 and 2.5, students will hopefully see patterns emerge. For example, when multiplying 8 by a number to get a response less than 4, students should begin to see that the number is often a fraction less than one-half and greater than or equal to zero. If students think "outside the box," they may also consider negative numbers, since any negative number multiplied by 8 will result in a number less than 4. Teachers, of course, should encourage this type of thinking.

# Common Factors and Common Multiples

## Grade 6

The notions of *greatest common factors* and *least common multiples* can be difficult for students to grasp, particularly because the language used to describe these concepts is often unfamiliar to them. For example, to most students the word "greatest" takes on the meaning of "best," and not the somewhat outdated meaning of "largest." Students often put the words "least common" together to misinterpret the meaning of the statement as "not having much in common." Teachers should clarify that the term *greatest common factor* (usually abbreviated as GCF) means the "biggest" or "largest" of the factors shared by a pair or set of numbers, and that *least common multiple* (usually abbreviated as LCM) means the "smallest" of all of the multiples of a pair or set of numbers that are the same.

The following two tasks allow students to meet the standard 6.NS.4, "Find the greatest common factor of two whole numbers less than or equal to 100 and the least common multiple of two whole numbers less than or equal to 12" (NGA Center and CCSSO 2010, p. 42). Task 2.7 gives students a context in which to consider common factors, and eventually the greatest common factor. Task 2.8 provides a context for common multiples.

## Task 2.7

Saheed has 16 vegetable plants and 24 flower plants and is making trays of plants for the school plant sale. Each tray must have the same number of plants, but only one type of plant per tray, and all the plants must be used up.

(*a*) Can Saheed put 3 of each plant in a tray and use them all up? If not, why not? What are some possible numbers of plants that Saheed can place in each tray? Think of as many different possibilities as you can.

(*b*) Based on your answer in part (*a*), what is the largest number of plants Saheed can place in each tray, considering that all trays must have the same number of plants, each tray must have only one type of plant, and all the plants must be used up?

Notice that the word "largest" is used in part (*b*) instead of "greatest." Students may find it helpful to draw a picture to represent each tray or to use a concrete item to model each type of plant. The possible solutions for part (*a*) would be to place 1, 2, 4, or 8 plants in each tray. Students should be encouraged to examine the relationships among the numbers of plants given in the problem to begin to see the idea of *common factor.* There can be two plants per tray, since 2 "goes into" both 16 and 24. Similarly, there can be 4 in each tray, or 8 in each tray. Obviously, 8 is the largest number that can go into both 16 and 24, and therefore it the greatest common factor.

We can connect what was just done above to the distributive law. If there are 2 plants of the same type per tray, then there are 8 trays of vegetable plants using up 2(8) plants, and 12 trays of flower plants using up 2(12) plants. So we have used up 2(8) + 2(12) plants. Of course, the number of plants used up can also be counted as follows: 2 of each plant in each of the (8 + 12) trays. The statement 2(8 + 12) = 2(8) + 2(12) models the situation. Of course, this is the distributive law. Similarly, 4(4 + 6) = 4(4) + 4(6) models the situation with 4 plants per tray, and 8(2 + 3) = 8(2) + 8(3) models it with 8 plants per tray. Discussion with students should lead them to see that the numbers "outside" the parentheses on the left side of these examples of the distributive law are all common factors of 16 and 24, with 8 being the largest of the common factors, or the "greatest" common factor. The expression with 8 as the common factor models the situation with the largest number of plants per tray. Students should also notice that when the "greatest" common factor is outside the parentheses, the numbers in parentheses have no common factors.

There are several ways in which task 2.7 may be modified in order to differentiate instruction. Larger or smaller numbers for each type of plant may be used in order to make the problem more or less difficult. Three (or even more) types of plants may be given in the problem in order to make the problem more challenging. For example, a teacher may decide that he or she would like students to find the greatest common divisor of 40, 48, and 88 and model the problem accordingly. Thus, a third type of plant would be needed, and there would be 40, 48, and 88 of each type of plant. A greatest common factor different from 8 could also be used. For another variation, based on the interest of the students, a context other than plants (candy, cupcakes, sports equipment, art tools, etc.) may be used. Finally, teachers may consider having students create their own problems. For example, students can be asked to write a problem with 2 plants in which the greatest number of plants per tray is 6, leading to a pair of numbers in which the GCF is 6.

Further, teachers may elect to give students more freedom in writing their own problems, without providing a value to use as the GCF. Of course, students can then solve each other's problems.

Task 2.8 provides students with a context in which to consider common multiples, and, eventually, the least common multiple.

## Task 2.8

Two pairs of friends are walking around the oval track in their schoolyard for an hour after school. They all begin at the beginning of the track and at the same time. The first pair takes 6 minutes to walk around the track once. The second pair takes 9 minutes to walk around the track once.

(*a*) After how many minutes will they meet again at the beginning of the track?

(*b*) If they walk for an hour, how many times will they meet at the beginning of the track?

Drawing a picture or making a list can help students to examine the constraints of this problem. Students may find it helpful to list the number of minutes it takes each pair to walk around the track. Pair 1 completes a walk after 6, 12, 18, 24, 30, 36, 42, 48, 54, and 60 minutes. Pair 2 completes a walk after 9, 18, 27, 36, 45, and 60 minutes. Therefore, they will meet at the beginning of the track after 18 minutes. Students should circle (or otherwise indicate) the numbers that are the same in both lists. They may notice that the numbers of minutes to each meeting at the beginning of the track are multiples of both 6 and 9, and they should be informed that these are called "common multiples" because these are the multiples that 6 and 9 have in common. The number of minutes that pass before the first meeting is the smallest (or "least") common multiple (LCM), and the other common multiples are themselves multiples of the LCM.

Similar to task 2.7, task 2.8 may be modified by using larger numbers for the amount of time that each pair takes to complete a walk around the track. Teachers may want to avoid numbers that are relatively prime (i.e., numbers that have no common factors other than 1), at least initially, so that students do not erroneously conclude that the LCM is always the product of the two given numbers. Another modification would be to have three (or more) pairs walking around the track, thus finding common multiples and the LCM of three or more numbers. As in task 2.7, students can also write their own LCM problems, and trade with each other to solve them.

### DISCUSSION—*Tasks 2.7 and 2.8*

Tasks 2.7 and 2.8 allow students to learn new mathematical concepts through solving unfamiliar problems. Students must first make sure they understand what the problems are asking, devise a plan to determine the solution, carry out the plan, and check whether or not their solution makes sense in the context of the original problem.

## MP.4

The contexts presented in each of the problems above are real-life situations that might be similar to those that students have experienced, thus giving them the opportunity to "model with mathematics." They must "analyze . . . relationships mathematically to draw conclusions" and "interpret their mathematical results in the context of the situation" (NGA Center and CCSSO 2010, p. 7).

## MP.5

In each of the above problems, students may decide to make lists for the important quantities in order to more easily visualize the common factors and multiples. Carefully structuring their lists in a sensible way so that the common factors and multiples are evident would be the result of "us[ing] appropriate tools strategically" (NGA Center and CCSSO 2010, p. 7).

## MP.7

In relating the numerical values in the problem, and in discovering how they relate to the solution to the problem, students are able to "look for and make use of structure" (NGA Center and CCSSO 2010, p. 8). By examining a list of the various multiples of the quantities in task 2.8, students can examine the structure of the lists of multiples of each number and see that the common multiples increase by a value equal to the least common multiple. Flexibility with this structure may help students to solve similar problems.

# Irrational Numbers

## Grade 8

The grade 8 standards for the Number System domain focus on developing understanding of irrational numbers. Students can gain firsthand experience with the exciting historical development of irrational numbers if it is introduced in relation to the Pythagorean theorem. Therefore, the task that follows should be done after the students have learned about the Pythagorean theorem. This next task supports standard 8.NS.2, which asks students to "use rational approximations of irrational numbers to compare the size of irrational numbers" and "locate them approximately on a number line" (NGA Center and CCSSO 2010, p. 54). Since the Pythagorean theorem is necessary for the problem, it also supports standard 8.G.8, "Apply the Pythagorean theorem to find the distance between two points in a coordinate system" (NGA Center and CCSSO 2010, p. 56).

Task 2.9 gives students a means to map irrational numbers that represent the lengths of the hypotenuse of right triangles to the *x*-axis, thus determining a rational approximation for the irrational number. When plotting the points that represent smaller numbers, students should be asked to use a scale on their graph paper such as 5 boxes equal 1 unit, or 4 boxes equal 1 unit, so that the values will be easy to estimate.

## Task 2.9

Plot the points (0, 0), (1, 0) and (1, 1) on the coordinate plane. (Use a scale so that 4 boxes equal one unit.)

(*a*) Connect the points to form a right triangle. Use the Pythagorean theorem to determine the exact length of the hypotenuse of the triangle.

(*b*) Use a compass to form a circle whose center is the origin and whose radius is the length of the hypotenuse. Examine where the circle intersects the *x*-axis (see fig. 2.3). What are the coordinates of this point? Label the point *R*.

(*c*) What are the integers that the *x*-coordinate of point *R* lies between? Using non-integer decimals, what are the approximate values for this coordinate?

(*d*) Use a calculator to find the rational approximation of the length you found in part (*a*). Was your estimate close?

(*e*) Repeat each of the above steps on a different pair of axes with the sets of points below. Label the points *S, T,* and *U*.

        (*i*)      (0, 0), (1, 0), (1, 2)
        (*ii*)     (0, 0), (1, 0), (1, 3)
        (*iii*)    (0, 0), (1, 0), (1, 4)

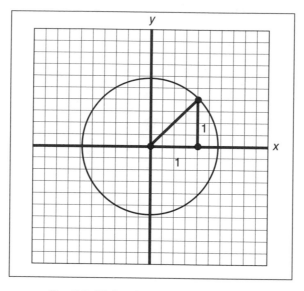

Fig. 2.3. Right triangle and circle from
parts (*a*) and (*b*)

Upon completion of all four parts of this problem, students will have four irrational numbers plotted on the *x*-axis, allowing them to see that irrational lengths are in fact real lengths that can be represented on the number line. Although this exercise is not a problem-solving situation, it can be used as a launch for a lesson on irrational numbers, their connection with the Pythagorean theorem, and a way to make rational approximations of irrational numbers. This allows for discussion between students and teachers about these conceptual ideas, and it sets the stage for further lessons involving irrational numbers. Teachers may, of course, give different sets of coordinates in order to approximate different irrational numbers.

## DISCUSSION—*Task 2.9*

As mentioned above, although this is not truly a problem-solving situation, it provides students the opportunity to make a discovery and make connections between different aspects of the number system.

**MP.5**

In using graph paper and a compass (or another device to make a circle), students are "us[ing] appropriate tools strategically" (NGA Center and CCSSO 2010, p. 7) in order to reveal the connection between irrational numbers and the real number line.

**MP.7**

When examining the relationships between the irrational lengths of the hypotenuses of the right triangles and the number line, students are "look[ing] for and mak[ing] use of structure" (NGA Center and CCSSO 2010, p. 8).

# Chapter 3
# Geometry

**M**iddle school teachers are presented with unique challenges when teaching geometry to their students as they transition to abstract geometric thinking. Prior to the middle grades, students have had a variety of experiences with geometric concepts. Students in earlier grades likely recognize shapes by their visual appearance (Schwartz 2013), while in later grades students should be moving toward recognizing a shape by observing and analyzing its properties. For example, students in earlier grades recognize a square as such because it matches their visual image of what a square should look like. Older students may determine a figure is a square by examining the figure and determining that it has the properties of a square.

Prior to the middle grades, students have also begun to work with various measurement concepts, including area, perimeter, and volume, along with other types of measurement. Even with those experiences, students entering the middle grades might not have a deep grasp of the concepts of the differences among linear measures, and of the differences between square and cubic units used for area and volume, respectively. Students typically have had experience with nonstandard units of measure, using physical items such as paper clips, edges of variously sized cubes, and even their hands or feet to measure length. Various nonstandard items such as index cards or their hands might have been used to measure area informally, and such items as packing peanuts or popcorn can be used to fill containers to develop the concepts of volume. It is important to emphasize area as a measure of "covering" and volume as a measure of "filling."

Nonstandard units of measure and their drawbacks motivate the need for standard units of measure, which begin with linear measure, with square and cubic units based on standard linear units, such as inches or centimeters. Because the metric system is based on the base-10 number system, it is easier to use than the traditional "British" system of measures commonly used in the United States.

Students in the middle grades are developing the ability to move away from the description of figures based upon their visual attributes and moving toward the examination of properties to determine the type of figure with which they are dealing. Teachers may be familiar with the levels of geometric thought developed by Pierre van Hiele and Dina van Hiele-Geldof. The "van Hiele levels" (Fuys, Geddes, and Tischler 1988) are summarized in table 3.1.

Table 3.1

*The van Hiele levels of geometric thought*

| Level | Description |
|---|---|
| Level 0 | Identifies, names, compares, and operates on geometric figures according to their appearance. (Visualization) |
| Level 1 | Analyzes figures in terms of their components and relationships among components and discovers properties/rules of a shape empirically (e.g., by folding, measuring, using a grid or diagram). (Analysis) |
| Level 2 | Logically interrelates previously discovered properties/rules by giving or following informal arguments. (Abstraction) |
| Level 3 | Proves theorems deductively and establishes interrelationships among networks of theorems. (Deduction) |
| Level 4 | Establishes theorems in different postulational systems and analyzes/compares these systems. (Rigor) |

Teachers may erroneously assume that most students in the middle grades are at or approaching level 2; there is, however, evidence that this is not always the case, and, in fact, some students even in ninth grade are only at level 0 or level 1. Interestingly, by the middle grades, the progression through the levels is dependent more on instruction than on age or maturity. It is possible to "teach" through the levels (Fuys, Geddes, and Tischler 1988). Thus, teachers of students in the middle grades should be especially mindful of the varying levels of their students.

The middle school standards for geometry include content that is developed and built upon from grade 6 through grade 8. The "big ideas" of the middle school geometry curriculum involve measurement (area and surface area, volume, and angles), relationships among figures leading to congruence and similarity, and the Pythagorean theorem. The specific standards for the grade 6 geometry domain are clustered under a single overarching standard, which is "Solve real-world and mathematical problems involving area, surface area, and volume" (National Governors Association Center for Best Practices [NGA Center] and Council of Chief State School Officers [CCSSO] 2010, p. 44). Grade 7 standards are expanded upon and clustered into two overarching standards: "Draw, construct, and describe geometrical figures and describe the relationships between them" and "Solve real-life and mathematical problems involving angle measure, area, surface area, and volume" (NGA Center and CCSSO 2010, p. 49–50). The geometry standards are further refined and clustered in grade 8, where students are asked to work with indirect measurement using the Pythagorean theorem along with notions of similarity and congruence. The overarching grade 8 standards are "Understand congruence and similarity using physical models, transparencies, or geometry software"; "Understand and apply the Pythagorean theorem"; and "Solve real-world and mathematical problems involving volume of cylinders, cones, and spheres" (NGA Center and CCSSO 2010, p. 55–56). Through the middle grades, the standards evolve to ensure that students are ready to meet the challenges of high school geometry, including the notions of conjecture and proof.

What follows are six tasks to support area, surface area, and volume (tasks 3.1, 3.2, and

**34**

3.3), area and circumference of a circle, and the Pythagorean theorem (tasks 3.4a, 3.4b, and 3.5). The eight Standards for Mathematical Practice (MP), which are listed on page vi, are woven throughout these domains. Depending on the problem, a subset of those standards is discussed. We believe that all of the problems require "attention to precision," thus developing mathematically proficient students as required by the sixth Standard for Mathematical Practice. The tasks in this chapter are summarized in table 3.2.

Table 3.2
*Content areas, grade levels, and standards met by the tasks in chapter 3*

| Content Areas | Tasks | Grade 6 Standards | Grade 7 Standards | Grade 8 Standards | Standards for Mathematical Practice |
|---|---|---|---|---|---|
| Area in coordinate plane | 3.1 | 6.G.1, 6.G.3 | 7.G.6 | | MP.2, MP.3, MP.7 |
| Volume of right prisms | 3.2 | 6.G.3 | 7.G.3 | | MP.2, MP.3, MP.7 |
| Volume of right prism, cones, cylinders, and spheres | 3.3 | | 7.G.6 | 8.G.9 | MP.1, MP.4 |
| Area, perimeter, circumference, ratio, and percent | 3.4 | | 7.G.4, 7.G.6, 7.RP.3 | 8.G.7 | MP.1, MP.4 |
| Area, circumference | 3.5 | | 7.G.4 | | MP.1, MP.4 |

# Area, Surface Area, and Volume

## Grades 6 and 7

The first task in this chapter requires that students plot points on the coordinate plane, find the area of the triangle that is formed by the coordinates, and modify the problem according to two student errors that transform the given problem into a more difficult one, requiring composition into a rectangle in order to determine the area of the new shape. Prior to solving the problems presented in the tasks, students should have experiences with the development of the formulas for the area of rectangles, parallelograms that are not rectangles, triangles, and trapezoids. As described in *Principles and Standards for School Mathematics*, students in the middle grades should have the opportunity to develop the formulas for the area of parallelograms, triangles, and trapezoids based on their knowledge of how to find the area of a rectangle, along with the knowledge that decomposing and rearranging a shape does not change the area of the shape (NCTM 2000, p. 244). NCTM's Illuminations website provides resources for this development of area formulas, along with online tools at http://illuminations.nctm.org/LessonDetail.aspx?ID=U160.

The problem that follows addresses two grade 6 geometry standards and part of one grade 7 standard. Standard 6.G.1 requires that students "find the area of right triangles, other triangles, special quadrilaterals, and polygons by composing into rectangles or decomposing into triangles and other shapes" (NGA Center and CCSSO 2010, p. 44). Standard 6.G.3 requires that students do the following: "Draw polygons in the coordinate plane given coordinates for the vertices; use coordinates to find the length of a side joining points with the same first coordinate or the same second coordinate. Apply these techniques in the context of solving real-world and mathematical problems" (NGA Center and CCSSO 2010, p. 45). Standard 7.G.6 asks that students "solve real-world and mathematical problems involving area, volume and surface area of two- and three-dimensional objects composed of triangles, quadrilaterals, polygons, cubes, and right prisms" (NGA Center and CCSSO 2010, p. 50).

## Task 3.1

(a)  Plot the points $A$ (2, 5), $B$ (8, 1), and $C$ (2, –3) on the coordinate plane, and connect them to form triangle $ABC$. Calculate the area of triangle $ABC$. Explain your work.

(b)  Sean solves the problem above and compares his work with his friend, and he notices that his answer is different. In checking his work, he realizes that he plotted the first two points correctly, but he plotted point $C$ at (–2, –3) instead of (2, –3). What is the area of the shape that Sean plotted?

(c)  Why is the area of Sean's shape more difficult to calculate? Explain.

(d)  Jesse noticed that she plotted point $B$ incorrectly but the area of her triangle is still correct. Where could Jesse have plotted point $B$?

This problem allows for several extensions and modifications. In parts (b) and (c), Sean's problem is more difficult because none of the sides of the triangle are parallel to the x-axis or y-axis, and the triangle that he draws must be inscribed in a rectangle and the areas of triangles *ACD, AEB,* and *BFC* subtracted from the area of rectangle *CDEF* in order to calculate the triangle's area (see fig. 3.1).

In part (d), Jesse plotted point $B$ incorrectly but her area is correct. The goal of this part of the problem is to have students recognize that the height of the triangle is the same as the correctly plotted triangle, thus not changing the area. Therefore, the point $B$ that Jesse plotted must have an x-coordinate equal to 8, but a different y-coordinate. There are infinitely many points that meet this requirement. Students can examine coordinates for a point $B$ in which the height falls outside the triangle, "shearing" the triangle but keeping the base and height, and thus the area, the same.

The number of coordinates given can be increased, thus allowing for a variety of polygons to be drawn and their areas calculated, and leading to a problem that might require decomposition of the shape into simpler shapes. For example, students could be asked to plot *A* (4, 10), *B* (6, 10), *C* (6, 5), *D* (9, 5), *E* (9, 2), *F* (1, 2), *G* (1, 5), and *H* (4, 5) and connect the points to form octagon *ABCDEFGH*. Students must decompose the figure into two rectangles to determine the area of the polygon (see fig. 3.2).

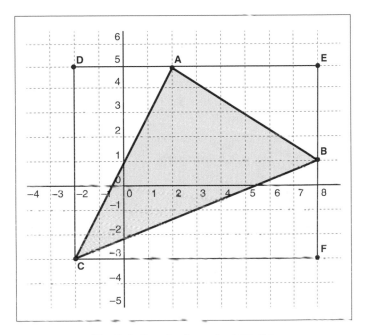

Fig. 3.1. Sean's shape for task 3.1

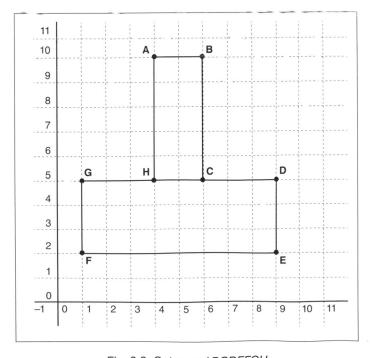

Fig. 3.2. Octagon *ABCDEFGH*

Segment $AB$ can also be shifted to the left or right, shearing the polygon without changing the area. For example, the coordinates can be changed to $A$ (11, 10) and $B$ (13, 10). Students may find it counterintuitive that this change does not change the area of *ABCDEFGH*. They might be asked to generalize the coordinates of points $A$ and $B$ that similarly shear the octagon but do not change the area of the figure, which would be in the algebraic form $A$ ($k$, 10) and $B$ ($k$ + 2, 10) for any $k$. Students might find it surprising that the area is the same as that of the original shape for any value of $k$.

Similarly to what happened in part (*b*) of the given problem, an intentional "mistake" can be made that modifies the problem to include fewer segments that are parallel to the *x*-axis or *y*-axis; this makes the problem more difficult and requires students to "box in" the triangle and subtract areas to find the solution.

The next activity uses pattern blocks and their properties to examine and analyze aspects of volume informally, addressing the part of CCSSM standard 6.G.2 that states "Apply the formulas $V = lwh$ and $V = Bh$ to find volumes of right rectangular prisms" (NGA Center and CCSSO 2010, p. 45). It also sets the stage for meeting standard 7.G.3, "Describe the two-dimensional figures that result from slicing three-dimensional figures, as in plane sections of right rectangular prisms and right rectangular pyramids" (NGA Center and CCSSO 2010, p. 50). This problem requires defining and using a nonstandard unit of volume (the green triangular pattern block) to develop the formula $V = Bh$. The goal is to emphasize that volume is a function of the base and the height of a solid. Since the green triangular block has a volume of 1, we can conclude that the blue rhombus block has a volume of 2 cubic units, the red trapezoid block has a volume of 3 cubic units, and the yellow hexagon block has a volume of 6 cubic units. The height is the "thickness" of the block, which we consider to be 1 unit (see fig. 3.3 for an illustration of the pattern blocks). The goal of this problem is to build conceptual understanding of the components of volume. The blocks all have the same thickness, which should be considered as one unit of height. For this activity, the square blocks and small rhombi blocks will not be used. Rectangular prisms will be formed by stacking congruent pattern blocks according to the constraints of the problem.

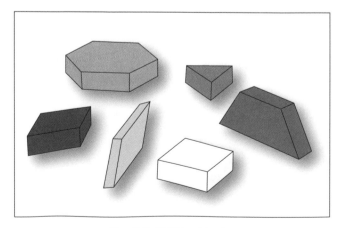

Fig. 3.3. Pattern blocks

# Task 3.2

(*a*) Using the green triangular block as the base, create a triangular prism that has a volume of 12 cubic units. Sketch what you have constructed. What is the height of the solid you have constructed?

(*b*) Using the blue rhombus block as a base, create a rhomboid prism that has a volume of 12 cubic units. Sketch what you have constructed. What is the height of the solid you have constructed?

(*c*) Using the red trapezoidal block as the base, create a trapezoidal prism that has a volume of 12 cubic units. Sketch what you have constructed. What is the height of the solid you have constructed?

(*d*) Create two prisms that have the same volume but that have different bases. How would you explain to a friend that the volumes are the same? Sketch what you have created.

(*e*) Create two prisms in which one has a volume that is three times the other, while both have the same height.

This task is intended to give students an intuitive feel for the important measurements that are involved in the calculation of volume. When the area of the base of one prism is half the area of the base of another prism, students should see that the height of the prism with the larger base is half the height of the prism with the smaller base. Throughout the activity teachers should emphasize that volume is a function of the area of the base multiplied by the height. Since task 3.2 allows students to work with nonstandard units of volume, teachers might want to follow up this activity with reintroducing the formula for finding the volume of a right rectangular prism. This link to the Illuminations website provides an opportunity to work with this formula: http://illuminations.nctm.org/ActivityDetail.aspx?ID=6. Again, it should be emphasized that the volume is the area of the base of the box multiplied by the height of the box.

## DISCUSSION—*Tasks 3.1 and 3.2*

Tasks 3.1 and 3.2 facilitate the development of mathematically proficient students by allowing them to meet several of the CCSSM Standards for Mathematical Practice through problem solving. Students must make sure that they understand what is being asked in the problem, make a plan for how to solve the problem, and apply a strategy. An appropriate strategy for task 3.1 might be to "draw a picture" and "use direct reasoning." When solving this problem, students need to assess the given information, synthesize what they know about the coordinate plane with what they know about area, and evaluate mistakes some fictional students have made and their impact on the problem and its difficulty level. A strategy that might be successful for task 3.2 is to "work backwards," "use a model," or "guess and check." For both problems, students can revisit their approaches in order to check their work and determine whether their solutions make sense. The following Standards for Mathematical Practice are targeted by these two tasks.

## MP.2

The design of tasks 3.1 and 3.2 allows students to "reason abstractly and quantitatively" (NGA Center and CCSSO 2010, p. 6). By asking students to evaluate the problem in task 3.1 as given and with a change that renders the problem more difficult, students must decontextualize and recontextualize, and they must determine what impact the change has on the problem and how and why the change makes the problem more difficult. Task 3.2 requires that students think deeply about the relationships among the base of the solid, the height of the solid, and its volume. Students must reason abstractly when changing certain dimensions while the volume remains constant.

## MP.3

When responding to the fictional students regarding their "mistakes" in task 3.1, students are "construct[ing] viable arguments and critiqu[ing] the reasoning of others" (NGA Center and CCSSO 2010, p. 6). Students must be able to analyze the mistakes made by each of the students and, in parts (*b*) and (*c*), figure out why the problem is more difficult based on what might seem like a simple error. In part (*d*), students must be able to determine under what conditions the point could be plotted incorrectly and still not change the area. Part (*d*) of task 3.2 asks students to explain to a friend that the volumes of the different solids are the same by creating a viable argument.

## MP.7

When solving the problem in task 3.1, students must "look for and make use of structure" (NGA Center and CCSSO 2010, p. 8). Specifically, they need to notice that calculating the area of a triangle on the coordinate plane is more difficult when none of the three sides are parallel to the axes. Students should also notice that line segments that are parallel to one of the axes have either *x*-coordinates that are equal, or *y*-coordinates that are equal. Further, students must recognize that any vertex that does not change the base or the height of the original triangle does not change the area of the original triangle.

Students are also "look[ing] for and mak[ing] use of structure" (NGA Center and CCSSO 2010, p. 8) when analyzing and calculating the volumes in task 3.2 that meet the constraints of the problem. In particular, students must analyze the structure of the relationship between the volume of a solid and the area of its base and its height. Students should observe that if the volume remains constant, and the height is multiplied by $n$, then the area of the base is divided by $n$.

# Grades 7 and 8

Prior to using the formulas for the volume of cones, cylinders, and spheres, students need to be given the opportunity to develop the formulas based on prior knowledge. An opportunity to develop the volume formula for a sphere is presented by Urich and Sasse (2011), where students develop the formula using sections of oranges. Students can derive the formula for the volume of a cylinder using the activity available at the NCTM Illuminations website at http://illuminations.nctm.org/LessonDetail.aspx?id=L797. They can determine the relationship between the volume of a cone and the volume of a cylinder with the same base and height by modeling each using paper, and experimenting with how many cones filled with beans can fit into the cylinder (see http://illuminations.nctm.org/FamilyGuide/FamilyGuide_FamiliesAsk.pdf).

Additionally, in preparation for task 3.3, which requires that students put together difficult ideas involving volume in a real-life water displacement problem, it might be helpful to give students an historical sense of how this situation might have come about. The following anecdote might capture students' attention (Allen 1980; also see http://www.math.wichita.edu/history/men/archimedes.html; http://www.math.nyu.edu/~crorres/Archimedes/Crown/CrownIntro.html).

> Archimedes of Syracuse (287–212 B.C.) was one of the most celebrated mathematicians and scientists of all time. A story is told of King Hiero II, who provided a jeweler with gold to make a crown for him. The crown was very ornate, but the king did not trust that all the gold he gave to the jeweler was used for the crown, and began to suspect that the jeweler had adulterated the gold with some other metal, perhaps silver. He asked Archimedes to determine whether the crown was made of real gold or some mixture of gold with another metal. Archimedes thought about this a long time and could not figure out how to determine whether this was real gold or not, without melting down the crown. One day in the bathtub it dawned on him that when he sat in the tub, the water rose, and must have been displaced by his volume. This gave him the idea of determining the volume of the crown by immersing it in water. From this information, he could determine whether the density of the object, mass divided by volume, was the same as pure gold. Legend has it that he was so excited by this discovery that he ran through the streets naked yelling "Eureka" (i.e., "I found it"). From this, he was in fact able to determine that the crown was not made of pure gold and that the jeweler had in fact taken some of the gold.

For an application of the principle that when a body is submerged in water, it displaces an amount of water equal to its volume, consider task 3.3. This task builds on previously learned concepts of volume, and it addresses standard 7.G.6, "Solve real-world and mathematical problems involving area, volume and surface area of two- and three-dimensional objects composed of triangles, quadrilaterals, polygons, cubes, and right prisms" (NGA Center and CCSSO, p. 50). A modification will be suggested so that the problem meets standard 8.G.9, "Know the formulas for the volumes of cones, cylinders, and spheres and use them to solve real-world and mathematical problems" (NGA Center and CCSSO 2010, p. 56).

## Task 3.3

Jennifer and her friends were bored one day and were playing with a tank of water whose dimensions were 48 centimeters long, 30 centimeters wide, and 36 centimeters high (see fig. 3.4a). They had some heavy, solid box-shaped items that had a 12 x 12-centimeter square base and were 20 centimeters tall. They put water in the tank so that it was 28 centimeters deep (not shown in the diagram), and started carefully dropping the box-shaped items into the tank and watching them fall to the bottom to see how many they could fit into the tank before it overflowed.

(a) When Jennifer and her friends put one box on the bottom of the tank, how many centimeters did the water rise?

(b) How many of the items could they put in the tank before it overflowed?

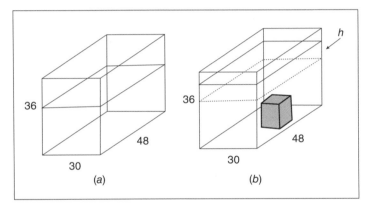

Fig. 3.4. Before (*a*) and after (*b*) items were dropped into
the tank of water

The solution of part (*a*) requires students to calculate the volume of the box we are putting in the tank, which is 2,880 cubic centimeters. This is also the volume of the water the box will displace. (See fig. 3.4a, showing what happens before we put the box in, and fig. 3.4b, which shows the situation after the box is submerged.)

If the height of the water rises by $h$ (see fig. 3.4b), then the volume of the water displaced (that part between the dotted rectangle and the solid rectangle in figure 3.4b) is equal to length times width times height, or 48 times 30 times $h$, which is 1,440$h$. Since this has to be 2,880 cubic centimeters, the value of $h$ is 2, and so 1 box will make the water level rise by 2 centimeters. Since the addition of each box raises the height of the water by 2 centimeters, there is a maximum of 4 items that may be placed in the tank without overflowing the tank.

Teachers may elect to modify this problem in several ways. Again, in part (*a*), teachers may ask how many centimeters *one* item will raise the water level. Further, since the volume of congruent solids raises the water level by the same amount, teachers may decide to give items that do not cause equal rises in the water level, making the problem more challenging. Teachers may also give a variety of items of different volumes in order for students to make the decision of what items to put in the tank, with the challenge of how many items can be placed on the bottom of the tank before the water overflows.

For the problem to directly address standard 7.G.6, the items need to be cubes or other right prisms. This problem may be modified to meet standard 8.G.9 by including items that are not right prisms, such as cones, cylinders, and spheres. Students should notice that if one puts only cones on the bottom of the tank, the number of cones one could put down without the water overflowing is approximately three times the number of cylinders that could be put down without overflow if only cylinders were used.

## DISCUSSION—*Task 3.3*

Students must use problem-solving strategies in order to be successful in solving these problems. In making a plan for solving the problem in task 3.3 in its original and modi-fied forms, students might consider drawing a picture of the tank in order to visualize better the problem. Making a table would also be useful in order to keep track of the different volumes and surface areas that arise in the problem.

### MP.1

Given the nature of this problem, students must first make sense of the problem and persevere in order to solve it successfully. They must analyze the constraints and goals of the problem, making sense of the relationship between the volume of the tank and the volume of the water in the tank, and understanding the somewhat sophisticated idea of converting the volume of a solid to the number of centimeters the water level will rise when the solid is placed in the tank.

### MP.4

When solving this problem, students are modeling with mathematics. They are asked to analyze the situation given in a problem that they themselves might encounter. Students must sensibly examine the various volumes and measures given in the problem and apply the quantities to the real-life situation of the tank. Further, the problem on the grade 8 level requires that students use the ratio of the volume of cylinders and cones that have the same base and height, and that they think about how these quantities relate to the problem with water displacement.

# Area and Circumference of a Circle, and the Pythagorean Theorem

## Grades 7 and 8

The notions of area and circumference of circles are introduced in grade 7 by meeting standard 7.G.4, "Know the formulas for the area and circumference of a circle and use them to solve problems" (NGA Center and CCSSO 2010, p. 50). In order to see where the area and circumference formulas of a circle come from, students should be engaged in hands-on activities that allow them to measure the circumference and diameter of various circles and to examine the ratio of circumference to the diameter of each circle, noting that the ratio is always a bit more than 3. Once students are informed that Archimedes discovered that this ratio is a constant, and that the constant is π, students can then determine the general formula for the circumference of a circle algebraically. In order to develop the formula for the area of a circle, students can cut a circle into sectors of smaller and smaller size to relate the area of a circle to the area of a rectangle. These activities are available at the NCTM Illuminations site, http://illuminations.nctm.org/LessonDetail.aspx?ID=U159. With deep understanding of these relationships, students are able to solve problems using the formulas.

The Pythagorean theorem is introduced in grade 8 when students meet standard 8.G.7, "Apply the Pythagorean theorem to determine unknown side lengths in right triangles in real-world and mathematical problems in two and three dimensions" (NGA Center and CCSSO 2010, p. 56). Task 3.4 addresses standard 7.G.4 and, depending on the level of implementation, can incorporate the Pythagorean theorem, thus meeting standard 8.G.7. Task 3.4 also addresses standard 7.G.6, "Solve real-world and mathematical problems involving area, volume and surface area of two- and three-dimensional objects" (NGA Center and CCSSO 2010, p. 50). In particular, students are solving a real-world problem involving a square inscribed in a circle using the formulas for the area of a square and the area of a circle. The real-life problem involves percent increase as well, thus also peripherally addressing standard 7.RP.3, "Use proportional relationships to solve multistep ratio and percent problems" (NGA Center and CCSSO 2010, p. 48), including percent change problems.

The problem is presented with two versions, one with numerical values and one without. Included in the version with numerical values are suggestions for scaffolding the problems. Version 1 is mainly appropriate for grade 8; version 2 can be modified to omit the Pythagorean theorem, thus rendering it a grade 7 problem.

## Task 3.4 (Version 1)

At a restaurant, a square table has flaps on it that can be raised to turn it into a round table. When the flaps are raised, both the area and the perimeter of the table are increased (see fig. 3.5). If four people can sit around the square table, how many do you expect could sit around the larger round table? What percent increase took place in the perimeter when the flaps were opened? How much area can each person use for himself or herself at the table (assuming the table is divided equally among them)? What is the percent increase of the area of the table with the flaps raised?

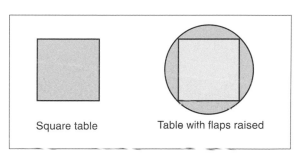

Fig. 3.5. Examples of tables in a restaurant

When implementing a problem on this level, scaffolding might be necessary. Questions could include: "What information would it be important to know in order to answer this question?" (area of circle, area of square); "How can we express this information?"; and "Should we choose a length for the side of the square? What would a convenient length be?" Alternatively, the question about percent increase can be omitted and students can simply be asked to make up their own questions about the situation. Although students are often asked to leave their solutions in "exact" form (in terms of $\pi$ or in radical form), the percent increase is more striking when using rational estimates for these numbers. Students might be asked whether they think that changing the size of the initial table would affect the percent increase. It is surprising that, regardless of the initial measurements of the table, the area increases by about 57 percent, while the circumference of the circle is only 11 percent greater than the perimeter of the square. Depending on the level of the students, teachers might prefer simply to ask students the ratio of the area of the square to the area of the circle, and the ratio of the perimeter of the square to the circumference of the circle. Only asking students to determine the ratios would avoid some somewhat lengthy, but not difficult, calculations. A more scaffolded version of this problem follows.

## Task 3.4 (Version 2)

At a restaurant, a square table has flaps on it that can be raised to turn it into a round table. The length of each side of the square table is four feet. Answer the following questions to determine the percent increase of the area and the perimeter (circumference) of the table with the flaps raised.

(*a*) What is the area of the square table?

(*b*) What is the perimeter of the square table?

(*c*) What is the diameter of the round table (the table with its flaps raised)? What is its radius?

(*d*) What is the area of the round table?

(*e*) What is the circumference of the round table?

(*f*) If we assume that 4 people can sit at the smaller square table and 6 people can sit at the larger round table, how much area can each person use and how much perimeter can each person use (assuming that everyone gets equal area and perimeter)?

(*g*) What percent increases took place in the area and perimeter when the flaps were opened?

If given to grade 7 students who have not yet worked with the Pythagorean theorem, teachers can give students the length of the diameter of the circle (which is the same task as the diagonal of the square), which, if the side of the square is 4 feet, would be approximately 5.66 feet by calculating the value of $4\sqrt{2}$. Again, if teachers prefer not to involve percent increase, they can ask students to determine the ratio of areas and the ratio of perimeters as described in the earlier version of the problem.

Task 3.5 presents a real-life situation that students might find familiar, one involving ordering pizza at a restaurant. It is also suitable for meeting standard 7.G.4, "Know the formulas for the area and circumference of a circle and use them to solve problems" (NGA Center and CCSSO 2010, p. 50).

# Task 3.5

According to the menu at Corner Pizza, a 12-inch pie costs $10, and an 18-inch pie costs $20. Isabella complains to the owner, "The diameter of the larger pie is $1\frac{1}{2}$ times the diameter of the smaller pie, but the price is double that of the smaller pie. That's a rip-off! So it's better to get two smaller pizzas than one larger pizza. You will get more for the same price."

The owner answers, "On the contrary, my friend. The larger pie has more than double the pizza the smaller pie has."

(*a*) Who is right? Explain.

(*b*) If pizza costs a fixed amount per square inch, what is the approximate cost per square inch of the smaller pie?

(*c*) If the larger pizza costs the same amount per square inch as the smaller pizza, approximately what would be the price of the larger pie?

Task 3.5 is designed to target some common misconceptions regarding area. Students must realize that, although the diameter of the larger pizza is 50 percent larger than the diameter of the smaller pizza, the area of the smaller pizza is only $36\pi$ square inches, while the area of the larger pizza is $81\pi$ square inches, more than twice the area of the smaller. Students must recognize that understanding the impact the radius has on the area of a circle is essential to understanding the problem.

## DISCUSSION—*Tasks 3.4 and 3.5*

The problems in the two versions of task 3.4 and the problem in task 3.5 allow the opportunity for students to solve problems in what is likely a very new situation, synthesizing different mathematical concepts to answer the questions in the task. Students must first understand what each of the problems is asking, and then determine a plan for calculating the various values and important quantities needed to make the necessary calculations. Since version 2 of task 3.4 scaffolds the problem, it requires the students to do a bit less, although the difficulty level of the problem is still quite high.

### MP.1

Because of the challenging nature of tasks 3.4 and 3.5, students must fulfill the first Standard for Mathematical Practice, which asks them to "start by explaining to themselves the meaning of a problem and looking for entry points to its solution" (NGA Center and CCSSO 2010, p. 6). Teachers, through careful questioning, can ensure that students do not give up on the problems and persevere until they reach a solution. Teachers should be mindful of not giving away too much information that would lower the difficulty level of the problem.

### MP.4

The real-life nature of these problems allows students to "model with mathematics" (NGA Center and CCSSO 2010, p. 7). Students may have seen such a table in their homes and would be curious about how much bigger the table becomes (in both area and circumference) with the flaps lifted. Similarly, students are usually quite familiar with purchasing a pizza. The problem in task 3.5 gives students a real-life opportunity to determine the important measures in figuring out how much pizza one gets, and to learn that changes in radius and diameter have an unexpected effect on the area of a circular object.

# Chapter 4
# Statistics and Probability

**M**ore than a century ago, in his book *Mankind in the Making*, H. G. Wells predicted that statistical reasoning would become as important as reading and writing for an educated citizen (1903/2004). Nevertheless, it is only within the past twenty-five years that statistics and probability have been included as a strand in the mainstream mathematics curriculum. Although the links between them are not always emphasized, statistics and probability work in tandem as they both focus on real-world phenomena that involve uncertainty.

Whether they realize it or not, statistics and probability are topics that permeate the lives of all middle school students. Teachers face challenges in trying to motivate students in grades 6–8 who are undergoing significant physical, emotional, and cognitive changes. Much of this difficulty can be overcome by finding out students' interests and then exploring the many statistical and probabilistic representations that will help them better understand and analyze situations that are of interest to them. Students' interests in games, food, styles, music, celebrities, sports, travel, video games, Twitter, and Facebook can be rich contexts to investigate. Today, with the help of technology, real-time data can be captured easily by posting a simple question on Google. Our role as teachers is to help students learn how to evaluate and interpret the data they capture and make informed decisions based on it.

The Common Core State Standards for Mathematics (CCSSM) develop the standards for this content in statistics and probability across grades 6 through 8. There are two clusters of standards in grade 6: "Develop understanding of statistical variability" and "Summarize and describe distributions" (National Governors Association Center for Best Practices [NGA Center] and Council of Chief State School Officers [CCSSO] 2010, p. 45). The three clusters of standards in grade 7 require students to "use random sampling to draw inferences about a population," "draw informal comparative inferences about two populations," and "investigate chance processes and develop, use, and evaluate probability models" (NGA Center and CCSSO 2010, p. 50). Students begin to examine bivariate data in grade 8, with standards under a single cluster that requires students to "investigate patterns of association in bivariate data" (NGA Center and CCSSO 2010, p. 56). The tasks that follow for each grade are meant to exemplify how these standards may be achieved using a problem-solving approach, with suggestions for various implementations.

The tasks in this chapter support statistical variability and measures of center (tasks 4.1, 4.2, and 4.3), plotting and comparing data (tasks 4.2, 4.3, 4.5, and 4.6), inference (task 4.4), and scatterplots (tasks 4.7 and 4.8). The eight Standards for Mathematical Practice (MP), as listed on page vi, are woven throughout these domains. Depending on the problem, a relevant subset of these standards is discussed. As in other chapters, we believe that all of the problems require "attention to precision," thus developing mathematically proficient students as required by the sixth Standard for Mathematical Practice. The tasks in this chapter are summarized in table 4.1.

Table 4.1
*Content areas, grade levels, and standards met by the tasks in chapter 4*

| Content Areas | Task | Grade 6 | Grade 7 | Grade 8 | Mathematical Practice |
|---|---|---|---|---|---|
| Statistical variability and measures of center | 4.1 | 6.SP.1, 6.SP.3 | | | MP.3, MP.4, MP.5 |
| Plotting data | 4.2 | 6.SP.4, 6.SP.5 | | | MP.3, MP.4, MP.5 |
| Comparing data | 4.3 | 6.SP.4, 6.SP.5 | 7.SP.3, 7.SP.4 | | MP.3, MP.4, MP.5 |
| Inference | 4.4 | | 7.SP.1, 7.SP.2 | | MP.2, MP.4, MP.5 |
| Comparing data | 4.5 | | 7.SP.3 | 8.SP.1 | MP.1, MP.2, MP.4 |
| Comparing data | 4.6 | | | 8.SP.1, 8.SP.2 | MP.1, MP.2, MP.4 |
| Scatterplots | 4.7 | | | 8.SP.1, 8.SP.2, 8.SP.3, 8.F.4, 8.F.5 | MP.1, MP.2, MP.4 |
| Scatterplots | 4.8 | | | 8.SP.1, 8.SP.2, 8.SP.3, 8.F.4, 8.F.5 | MP.1, MP.2, MP.4 |

# Statistical Variability

## Grades 6 and 7

In task 4.1, students are given a seemingly simple question to answer: Which day of the week are airline tickets least expensive? (The idea for this problem was provided by the undergraduate mathematics students of one of the authors of this volume.) In examining the issues involved in solving this problem, students soon realize that the data they are provided with are interesting and that there are many ways to answer the question. For example, they might try to find different measures of central tendency as summaries of their data, which they can then compare; or they might find ways to represent and examine the full distributions of the data that would give them a clearer picture of the variability of the data. When examining graphical representations of data, students are challenged to engage in all levels of reading graphs (Curcio 1987). That is, they must be able to *read* the data displayed in a graph, *read between* the data, and *read beyond* the data. They are even asked to search for specific causes of variation in the data, which involves what Shaughnessy, Garfield, and Greer (1996) described as *reading behind* the data or graphs.

If teachers wish, this task can be expanded to be a unit project that students do in class, or elements of the task can be used in class to launch the lesson. Although teachers may use side examples, the main problem provides a focus for the entire unit. Teachers may have students use Internet search engines to have them collect data based on particular questions they might be interested in answering. The task as presented involves determining the cheapest day to fly to Los Angeles (LAX airport) from New York (JFK airport) in order to see movie stars, since currently approximately 80 percent of all movie stars live in Los Angeles (according to wiki.answers.com). Teachers may wish to have students collect their own data. In that case, teachers can simply ask their students such questions as "Does it cost the same amount of money to travel from JFK to LAX on different days of the week?" and "How can we investigate, in general, what is the cheapest day of the week to fly?" If students are to collect the data themselves, they can check flight prices every day at the same time for 12 weeks, getting 12 prices for each day of the week for nonstop economy class flights from JFK to LAX (regardless of airline or time of flight, using a site such as http://www.bing.com/travel/). Teachers may instead decide to have the students collect 12 prices a day for a week to see what the data look like, and then use the data in a table such as table 4.2.

Table 4.2
*Prices in dollars for airline tickets to fly from JFK to LAX*

| Week # | Monday | Tuesday | Wednesday | Thursday | Friday | Saturday |
|--------|--------|---------|-----------|----------|--------|----------|
| 1 | 378 | 470 | 516 | 541 | 541 | 511 |
| 2 | 343 | 258 | 319 | 379 | 379 | 436 |
| 3 | 358 | 288 | 389 | 506 | 551 | 628 |
| 4 | 445 | 298 | 349 | 379 | 379 | 319 |
| 5 | 358 | 278 | 319 | 379 | 379 | 319 |
| 6 | 358 | 298 | 319 | 379 | 379 | 319 |
| 7 | 358 | 288 | 319 | 379 | 379 | 319 |
| 8 | 358 | 288 | 319 | 399 | 439 | 319 |
| 9 | 393 | 288 | 339 | 439 | 379 | 319 |
| 10 | 378 | 298 | 319 | 379 | 379 | 349 |
| 11 | 358 | 324 | 349 | 449 | 449 | 449 |
| 12 | 428 | 428 | 449 | 519 | 519 | 449 |

Once the data have been collected, the teacher can lead a class discussion regarding the best ways to analyze the data to get the information they are looking for. Students will realize that, having collected the data, it is not so simple to answer the question of which day of the week tends to be the least expensive day to travel. They will discover that since there are many different prices that occur for one day, there is no simple way to compare the prices. That is, the variability of the data for each day's price makes this question rather complex. Using the questions in task 4.1, the teacher can help scaffold the discussion so that students come up with different ideas about central tendency. Teachers may also wish to use an applet such as the one available through NCTM's Illuminations website to examine the mean and median of their data sets: http://illuminations.nctm.org/ActivityDetail.aspx?ID=160.

In task 4.1, students examine how variability of the data makes the issue of comparison between data sets so challenging, meeting standard 6.SP.1, "Recognize a statistical question as one that anticipates variability in the data related to the question and accounts for it in the answers," and 6.SP.3, "Recognize that a measure of center for a numerical data set summarizes all of its values with a single number" (NGA Center and CCSSO 2010, p. 45).

Students are asked to select one number that represents the price of a ticket on a particular day. Teachers may decide to arrange the class into six groups, one for each of the days from Monday through Saturday, where each group has a different set of data corresponding to the day of the week, or else have different students work on different days of the week. Teachers may want students to explore part (*a*) before showing them parts (*b*) through (*e*) of the task.

## Task 4.1

Compile your data set of the different prices available each day for flights from your chosen origin to your chosen destination, and answer the following questions:

(*a*) Decide which price is most representative of your data set. How did you arrive at this price? Make sure you can convince others why you chose the one you did.

(*b*) Was there a price that appeared multiple times in your data set? What was it? Were there multiple prices that were repeated? What were they? Do you think that the price that occurred the most times (the mode) would best represent your data set? Why or why not? According to the mode values, which day of the week would be least expensive to travel?

(*c*) When the prices are put in increasing order, is there a number that is in the middle of your data set? How can you determine what it is? Find the middle number (median) of your data set. How did you do it? Present your findings to the class.

(*d*) Examine your data set without the highest and lowest values. How did removing your extreme values affect your mode? Your median? Explain.

(*e*) Given your result from part (*d*), would you say that the median really reflects *all* of the values in your set of data? Why or why not? What is another way of finding one number that could represent all of your numbers? Add up all of your numbers and divide by the number of numbers you have. Do you get a number that seems to represent all of the other numbers? Why or why not? Explain how it compares with the mode and the median that you calculated for this set of data.

Teachers may decide to compile the "centers" for the data in table 4.2, which, in the case of the given data, are found in table 4.3.

Table 4.3
*"Centers" for the data in table 4.2*

|  | Monday | Tuesday | Wednesday | Thursday | Friday | Saturday |
|---|---|---|---|---|---|---|
| **Mode** | 358 | 288 | 319 | 379 | 379 | 319 |
| **Median** | 358 | 293 | 329 | 389 | 379 | 334 |
| **Mean** | 376.08 | 317 | 358.75 | 427.25 | 429.33 | 394.67 |

It is likely that there will be variability in the methods students use to select their numbers. Given that this will make comparisons difficult, they may feel the need to select one measure of central tendency. Building on students' initial preferences for finding "mosts" and "middles" (Watson and Moritz 2000, p. 46), students can be encouraged to sort the data from least to most expensive, for easier examination. Some data sets might have multiple modes, making it problematic to pick one of them. Students should then be encouraged to check for the "middle" number, or median. By demonstrating how changing the extreme values will not change the medians, students will see the value of using another measure that reflects all of the values in the data sets, the mean, but which is more sensitive to extremes. Furthermore, if students have an even number of numbers, to find the median they will have to find the mean of the two numbers that are in the middle.

Depending on the data gathered, students may or may not be satisfied with their selections of the best day to travel. To arouse their need for a more visual representation of the data, students can be challenged to consider what might happen if the day they went to purchase their ticket, the highest cost was being posted. Ask them if they had considered these possibilities when forming their charts. How might they envision the data better?

Having learned about bar graphs and histograms, students might wish to plot their individual sets of data. Tools, such as the applet available through http://illuminations. nctm.org/ActivityDetail.aspx?ID=78 and http://illuminations.nctm.org/ActivityDetail. aspx?ID=204 can facilitate students' understanding of histograms, bar graphs, and other visual representations of data, and they can enter their own data sets using these tools. They may also enter their data into a graphing calculator, or they can work in their groups to draw their graphs on large chart paper to be displayed to the class. The question will soon arise about how students can compare the different histograms or other graphs. Some may suggest drawing back-to-back histograms, but this will only allow them to compare two sets of data. This provides the perfect segue to launch the following task, in which students learn about the box-and-whisker plot that will allow them to compare multiple data sets. Tasks 4.2 and 4.3 address standard 6.SP.4, "Display numerical data in plots on a number line, including dot plots, histograms, and box plots," and 6.SP.5, "Summarize numerical data sets in relation to their context" (NGA Center and CCSSO 2010, p. 45).

In task 4.2, students investigate a "mystery plot" (i.e., the box plot) and discover all of its properties and advantages. If students do not have access to a graphing calculator, teachers may be able to project the screen from a graphing calculator using an overhead or document projector. Applets such as the one available at http://illuminations.nctm.org/ActivityDetail.aspx?ID=77 may also be used.

## Task 4.2

(*a*)  Enter the flight prices for the day of the week your group is examining into a "list" on your graphing calculator. Then select the plot that has a horizontal box with lines coming out of the side. This is the "mystery plot."

(*b*)  Trace the plot and record the numbers you see, starting at the farthest left part of the graph and moving to the farthest right. You should have recorded, at most, 5 numbers. Of the numbers you got when you traced the graph, which ones look familiar to you? What are they? Explain. Which ones do not look familiar to you?

(*c*)  Examine any unfamiliar numbers in relationship to the extremes and the median. Work alone at first and then with your group members to figure out how they were calculated.

Teachers may decide to have students present their graphs to the class, considering such questions as: "Is there a line in the middle of the box? Why or why not?"; "Is there a line coming out of the left or right side? Why or why not?"; and "Approximately what percentage of the data lies within each section of your graph?"

Once students examine the data in relation to the resulting box plots that the calculator gives them, they should begin to see that the calculator uses 5 data points to create the plot: the minimum and maximum, the median, and the first and third quartiles (which are the medians of the lower half of the data and the upper half of the data, respectively). Students can then consider how to read these plots and create them by hand.

After gaining some familiarity with the box-and-whisker plot, the teacher can now raise the questions "How can we compare the different data sets representing the costs for airline travel on different days?" and "How can the box-and-whisker plots help us to do that?" In the task that follows, the students can first compare three data sets on the graphing calculator. Then, by drawing their graphs on large chart paper and using a common scale, they can see how they are able to compare all of the data sets (in our case, six). Beforehand, the teacher should draw a scale at the bottom of each large graph paper chart that encompasses the extreme values from the six data sets. Again, if a calculator is not available, the Illuminations applet mentioned above may be used. In addition to meeting the same grade 6 standards as task 4.2 (6.SP.4 and 6.SP.5), task 4.3 also addresses grade 7 standards 7.SP.3 and 7.SP.4, which require that students "draw informal comparative inferences about two populations" (NGA Center and CCSSO 2010, p. 50).

## Task 4.3

(*a*) In your graphing calculator, enter the data from the day of the week your group is examining, along with that from the next two days that other groups in the class are examining. (For example, if your group is the Tuesday group, you should enter data from Tuesday, Wednesday, and Thursday.) Create a box-and-whisker plot for each of the three days to appear in one window. Explain what you see. That is, does your original graph look the same? Why or why not? How does your original graph compare with the other graphs? Can you say which has the lowest costs? The greatest costs? Explain.

(*b*) Draw the box and-whisker plot for your data set on large chart graph paper, using a given scale drawn by your teacher.

(*c*) Along with the other groups, tape your chart onto the board, lined up with the others for ease of comparison.

Figures 4.1 and 4.2 show the comparison of box plots and a sample of student work.

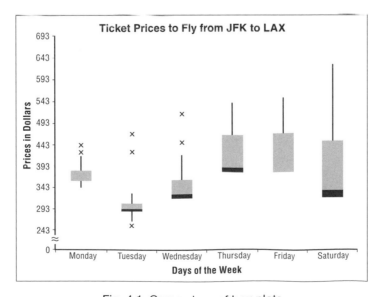

Fig. 4.1. Comparison of box plots

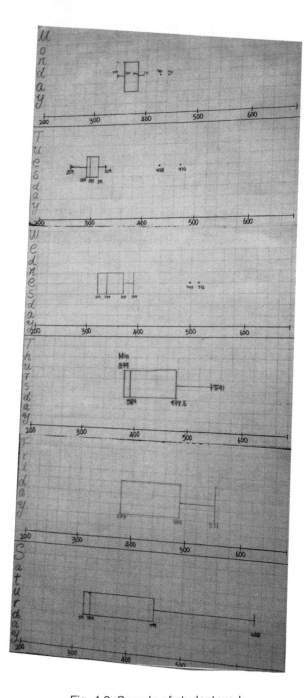

Fig. 4.2. Sample of student work

Once the box plots have been shared, the teacher can lead a discussion asking the students what they might attend to when deciding which day tends to be the least expensive day to travel. Answers to the following questions might be elicited:

- Which graph has the lowest extreme?
- Which graph has the highest extreme?

- Why do some of the graphs have two whiskers and others only one?
- Do all graphs show the median? Why or why not?
- Is the median ever in the middle of the box? Why or why not?
- What features of the graph would help you to decide which days are the least expensive or most expensive to travel?

## DISCUSSION—*Tasks 4.1 through 4.3*

The approaches used in the above three tasks allow for students to develop new knowledge through problem solving and discovery. Students must look at real-life data, which by its very nature is messy and disorganized, and determine ways to make sense out of it in order to answer important questions.

### MP.3

When determining the "best" number to describe the data in each set and deciding which numbers are familiar and which are less so in the above tasks, students must "construct viable arguments and critique the reasoning of others" (NGA Center and CCSSO 2010, p. 6). Tasks 4.1, 4.2, and 4.3 are rich with opportunities for students to convince their peers and teachers about the reasoning they used to make their decisions about the problems. Different students may make different decisions about the best day to fly based on their interpretation of the data, and they must be able to defend their decisions.

### MP.4

Using the real-life data that they collect themselves or that are provided for them gives students the opportunity to "model with mathematics." Specifically, they are "applying the mathematics they know to solve problems arising in everyday life, society, and the workplace" (NGA Center and CCSSO 2010, p. 7). These tasks provide a particularly rich opportunity for mathematical modeling because students may be determining the data to collect based on questions that they want to answer. They must interpret the graphs they make in the context of the questions they ask and within the limitations of the data they collect.

### MP.5

Whether using the Illuminations applet, a graphing calculator, or a hand drawing, students must determine which tools to use and how to use and interpret the results they get from them. Students should see why the scales change when the data are adjusted, and they should notice that the plots themselves may be seen as tools for data analysis.

# Inferential Statistics

## Grade 7

Questions regarding the practices, opinions, or conditions of the American people are often reported in newspapers and on the Internet. The tasks described below are designed to help students use a problem-solving approach when organizing, interpreting, and drawing conclusions about these sometimes conflicting sources of data, and when making predictions based on them.

Using real-life data that are relevant to students' lives is a good launching point for lessons involving sampling. A topic that has been forefront in the news for the past several years is the growing size of the average American. To begin the discussion, students might be asked whether they know the percentage of adults in the United States who are obese or overweight. (Although this is a national public health issue, we recognize the need for teachers to select topics that do not embarrass children. If desired, different data—such as eye color or population density—may be substituted using the same questions.) Some students might be able to share information that they have read on the Web, seen on TV, or heard from their families. After sharing their ideas, the teacher might question students about how these numbers were obtained. For example, were all adults in America weighed? Did all adults in America respond to a questionnaire? Were only some adults weighed or surveyed or interviewed? If so, how many and which people were included? Would it matter?

In preparation for the activity, students can be asked to conduct an Internet search for the percentage of overweight or obese Americans and to come to class with their results. They will undoubtedly have a great variety of results that bear analysis. The discussion can turn to the difficulty of gathering such data as these, and again, questions of sampling will arise. After discussing students' findings, the teacher can begin the activity by sharing the information reported by Hendrick (2010).

The Gallup-Healthways Well-Being Index reported that in 2009, 63.1 percent of adults in the U.S. were either overweight or obese (Hendrick 2010). It is explained in this report that the findings were based on telephone interviews with 673,000 adults. Given that there were approximately 218,000,000 adults in the United States at that time, only about 0.3 percent of the population was interviewed. This raises the question: How can surveying such a small percent of the population result in an accurate estimate of the entire population? The activity below is meant to model this type of situation and to help students understand the power and limitations of sampling. Students may work in pairs or small groups, and the teacher or a student can tally the results of each experiment. Of course, items other than jelly beans may be used, and teachers should emphasize that the jelly beans should be chosen without looking—that is, randomly. Alternatively, teachers may elect to create one bag that students pass around until every student has randomly chosen 15 jelly beans, which is a convenient sample with which to begin. Task 4.4 helps students to meet standard 7.SP.1, "Understand that statistics can be used to gain information about a population by examining a sample of the population" and

7.SP.2, "Use data from a random sample to draw inferences about a population" (NGA Center and CCSSO 2010, p. 50).

## Task 4.4

Imagine that 300 jelly beans represent the U. S. population. From this population, samples will be drawn. The 300 jelly beans are identical in size, but 100 of them are green and 200 are red. For this exercise, the 200 red jelly beans ($^2/_3$ of all of the jelly beans) will approximate the 63.1 percent of the population that is overweight or obese.

> (*a*) Choose 15 jelly beans from the bag *without looking.* Tally how many are red and how many are green.
>
> (*b*) Return the jelly beans to the bag and repeat part (*a*), again tallying how many red and green are chosen.
>
> (*c*) Write down your responses to the following questions:
>
> > (1) What did you expect would be the number of red jelly beans that would show up each time you chose 15 jelly beans?
> >
> > (2) Is it reasonable to expect that all of the samples taken during class will have that number of red jelly beans? Why or why not?
> >
> > (3) Is it possible that any of the samples drawn will contain all red jelly beans? Why or why not?
> >
> > (4) Would it be surprising if any of the samples drawn contained no red jelly beans? Why or why not?
> >
> > (5) Would it seem unusual to see 10 red jelly beans in one group of 15 chosen jelly beans? Why or why not?
> >
> > (6) What is a reasonable number of red jelly beans to expect when drawing a sample of size 15 from the given bag of 300 jelly beans?

As the results from each sample are reported, the teacher or a student should keep a tally of the number of samples of size 15 that have no reds, one red, two reds, three reds, and so on, up to 15 reds. From this tally a bar graph is constructed to depict the data. The sample bar graph in figure 4.3 depicts the results from a class of 26 students.

If the results in a class are similar to this typical distribution, students will see that most of the sample percents were somewhat close to the true population percent, which was 66.66 percent or $^{10}/_{15}$. In the example given in figure 4.3, none of the 26 samples contained fewer than 7 red jelly beans, although the percent of red jelly beans did vary from sample to sample. Eighteen of the 26 samples drawn (i.e., about 69 percent) contained 60 percent or 66.66 percent or 73 percent (i.e., 9, 10, or 11) red jelly beans; in other words, 69 percent of the samples were less than 10 percent away from the true population percent. Further discussion of these results will help students gain insight into the power and limitations of the data. For example, the students can be asked how their specific sample percents would have estimated the population percent. How likely is it that their estimate would be close to the true population percent of approximately 67 percent or $2/3$ that were red? Or, in terms of the original real-life problem, how well could they have used their sample to predict the actual percentage of people who were overweight or obese?

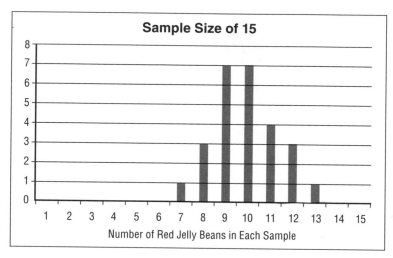

Fig. 4.3. A sample bar graph

Students can now be urged to consider a way to increase the chances of drawing a sample that would allow them to make an estimate that is close to the true population percent. It is hoped that they will suggest that increasing the size of the sample would improve the estimate. The teacher could then suggest that task 4.4 be repeated, but with a sample size of 30 instead of 15. Of course, question 5 in part (c) of task 4.4 should be changed to "Would it be unusual to see 20 red jelly beans in one group of 30 chosen jelly beans?" to reflect the changed sample size.

The bar graph in figure 4.4 gives an example of the results reached after increasing the sample size to 30. This time 19 of the 26 students (73 percent) selected samples that contained between 18 and 22 (60 to 73 percent) red jelly beans in the sample. This is an improvement from before, when 69 percent of the selected samples contained between 60 to 73 percent red jelly beans, and it demonstrates that an increase in the sample size resulted in an increase in the percent of samples that fell within 10 percent of the true population percent.

At this point, students might suggest increasing the sample size still further, which could become tedious were the jelly beans still to be used. This is a good opportunity to discuss the use of simulation and to try to elicit different methods that could be used to model this particular situation. The discussion would now link the concepts of data analysis and probability. This extension of the activity is designed to elicit how different simulations can be used to model ideas involving sampling, sample spaces, and the fact that in this situation, a successful experiment would yield a probability of $2/3$. Teachers could discuss different methods of simulating this experiment, including the use of a six-sided die, a spinner divided into three parts, a computer applet that generates integers from 1 to 6, a computer applet that represents a spinner with three parts, and an applet that simulates the toss of a six sided die. Questions similar to those in task 4.4 can be asked of students, with an emphasis on the fact that there must be a way to represent $2/3$ of the population. Students should be asked to simulate a sample of 60 cases and to again tally the number of successes. A spinner is provided at the NCTM Illuminations website: http://illuminations.nctm.org/ActivityDetail.aspx?ID=79. Any number of dice can be generated and rolled at http://www.random.org/dice/.

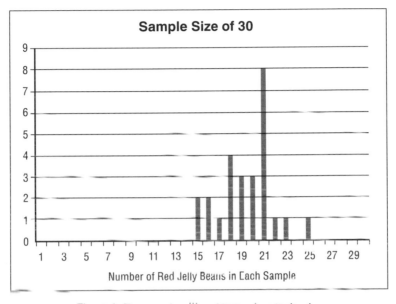

Fig. 4.4. Bar graph with increased sample size

## DISCUSSION—*Task 4.4*

The problem-solving approach taken in the simulation task above allows students to develop new knowledge through problem solving and to see that a simulation can act like a real experiment. Further, students will discover that as the number of trials increases, the experimental probability approaches the theoretical probability.

### MP.2

This real-life problem and its relationship to the various ways of simulating allow students the opportunity to "contextualize" the simulation and to "decontextualize" the real-life situation, thus "reason[ing] abstractly and quantitatively" (NGA Center and CCSSO 2010, p. 6). The questions asked in the task and its extension require students to relate the simulation to the real-life situation and to make a conjecture about the number of red jelly beans that would be expected to be chosen, and what that represents in the real-life context of the problem.

### MP.4

When using a simulation to represent the real-life situation presented in the problem, students are "model[ing] with mathematics"; specifically, they are "making assumptions and approximations to simplify a complicated situation," "identify[ing] important quantities in a practical situation," and analyzing "those relationships mathematically to draw conclusions" (NGA Center and CCSSO 2010, p. 7). They must decide what simulations are appropriate for the specific problem, and they should realize that any simulation they use must involve $2/3$ of one item and $1/3$ of another in order to accurately represent the real-life situation.

**MP.5**

When using computer simulations with dice, spinners, or randomly choosing jelly beans from a bag, students are "us[ing] appropriate tools strategically" (NGA Center and CCSSO 2010, p. 7). In addition to the simulations, they are also using graphic representations of their results, such as a bar graph, to visually represent the range of results that they obtain from each of the simulations. These tools facilitate understanding of the problem and understanding of the simulation, and its relation to the problem.

# Comparing Data

## Grades 7 and 8

Prior to grade 8, students have only had experience investigating univariate data, representing them through diagrams (e.g., histograms, bar graphs, line plots, stem-and-leaf plots, and box-and-whisker plots) and using measures of central tendency (e.g., mean, median, mode). It is not until grade 8 that students begin to study how two sets of univariate data may or may not be related, thereby studying bivariate data. For example, although students might have compared the distribution of heights of eighth graders in a school and the heights of mothers of eighth graders in a school, they have not done a pairing of the heights of specific students and their mothers. They have also not yet related two different types of data sets. For example, could there be a relationship between the heights of students and how much they exercised each week? To make the transition from the analysis of univariate to bivariate data analysis, teachers can begin by examining two sets of univariate data with the same units separately and then move to examining them together as bivariate data. They can then introduce bivariate data with different units of measure. The tasks that follow exemplify that transition. Any data set that is of interest to students can be used. In fact, it is often best if students collect their own data. Suggestions will be given in these tasks for data that might be collected or used. Our context is only used as a model for how the series of instruction and tasks could take place.

The first of these tasks engages students in an activity where they compare two data sets that use the same unit of measure—temperature in Fahrenheit degrees—for two different locations on the east coast of the U.S.: New York, New York, and Orlando, Florida. (Of course, locations may be changed based on the actual location and interests of the students performing the task.) As most students have taken, or at least wished to have taken, trips to Orlando, Florida, to visit the various theme parks located there, they are likely to be aware that the weather in Florida is usually warmer than in New York. Some students might also have relatives who have retired or moved to Florida, and they might be interested in knowing how the weather in Florida compares to that in New York. This task targets the grade 7 standard 7.SP.3, "Informally assess the degree of visual overlap of two numerical data distributions with similar variabilities" (NGA Center and CCSSO 2010, p. 50). This task also can serve as a review for grade 8 students, and it sets the stage for standard 8.SP.1, "Construct and interpret scatter plots for bivariate measurement data to investigate patterns of association between two quantities" (NGA Center and CCSSO 2010, p. 56).

Some of the discussion leading up to the task may include such questions as "How do you think the average temperature outside varies from one month to the next during a one-year period in New York?"; "Do you think it stays within 20 degrees Fahrenheit from one month to the next?"; "Do you think there are big deviations from month to month?"; and "Do you think it gets consistently warmer as the months progress from January to May?" The teacher may wish to gather students' guesses and predictions for these questions. In implementing the task, teachers may decide to have different groups of students work on part (*b*) and part (*c*) separately.

## Task 4.5

(*a*) Do you think the temperature stays within 20 degrees Fahrenheit from one month to the next in Orlando, Florida? In New York, New York? Do you think there are big deviations from month to month in each location? Do you think it gets consistently warmer as the months progress from January to July? Do you think it gets consistently colder as the months progress from August to December? Do you expect the weather patterns to be the same in Orlando and New York?

(*b*) Using the data in table 4.4, create a line graph for the average monthly temperature for New York. Be sure that the *x*-axis consists of the consecutive months and that they are labeled as integers from 1 to 12. The *y*-axis should be labeled as New York temperatures in Fahrenheit, and it should encompass the range of temperatures that appears in the data.

Table 4.4
*Average monthly temperature in degrees Fahrenheit in New York, New York*

| Annual | JAN | FEB | MAR | APR | MAY | JUN | JUL | AUG | SEP | OCT | NOV | DEC |
|--------|-----|-----|-----|-----|-----|-----|-----|-----|-----|-----|-----|-----|
| 55 | 32 | 34 | 43 | 53 | 63 | 72 | 77 | 76 | 68 | 58 | 48 | 37 |

*Source:* http://www.weatherbase.com/weather/weather.php3?s=330527&refer=&cityname=New-York-New-York-United-States-of-America

(*c*) Create a line graph on a different set of axes for the average monthly temperature for Orlando, using the data in table 4.5. Be sure that the *x*-axis consists of the consecutive months and that they are labeled as integers from 1 to 12. The *y*-axis should be labeled as Orlando temperatures in Fahrenheit and encompass the range of temperatures that appears in the data.

Table 4.5

*Average monthly temperature in degrees Fahrenheit in Orlando, Florida*

| Annual | JAN | FEB | MAR | APR | MAY | JUN | JUL | AUG | SEP | OCT | NOV | DEC |
|---|---|---|---|---|---|---|---|---|---|---|---|---|
| 72.4 | 61 | 61.9 | 66.1 | 71.8 | 77.4 | 81 | 82.4 | 82.5 | 80.8 | 74.9 | 66.8 | 61.8 |

*Source:* http://www.weatherbase.com/weather/weather.php3?s=150227&refer=&cityname=Orlando-Florida-United-States-of-America

(*d*) Write a few sentences that describe the data and explain your response regarding the variability of the temperature from one month to another during a full year and from January to May.

The line graphs described in parts (*b*) and (*c*) are shown in figures 4.5 and 4.6, respectively.

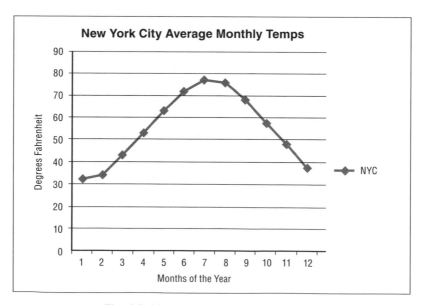

Fig. 4.5. Line graph for task 4.5, part (*b*)

At the conclusion of task 4.5, the teacher may ask the students how they might more easily compare the two line graphs. Some students might suggest graphing both on the same pair of axes. They might discuss how drawing such a double line graph would help them notice relationships that were previously more difficult to detect. Students could also be asked, in fact, to predict how the lines would appear (e.g., Would they intersect? Would they be parallel? Would one graph be higher than the other?). This leads to the next task, which addresses grade 8 standard 8.SP.1 as task 4.5 did, as well as standard 8.SP.2, "Know that straight lines are widely used to model relationships between two quantitative variables" (NGA Center and CCSSO 2010, p. 56).

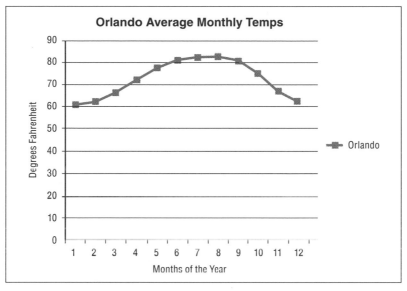

Fig. 4.6. Line graph for task 4.5, part (c)

# Task 4.6

(a) Create a double line graph using your data for New York average monthly temperatures and Orlando average monthly temperatures.

(b) Do your graphs intersect at any point? If they did, what would that mean? If not, what would that mean?

(c) Write a few sentences describing your double line graph.

The graph in figure 4.7 shows the completed double line graph.

In order to elicit the idea of scatterplots, students might be queried (after extensive analyses of the two line plots) how they might more clearly represent the relationship of the two sets of data. Might there be a way to do it that would help us to envision it more readily? If students have not already thought of it, ask them to create a table where the temperatures are paired. Then elicit the idea that each month's average temperature could be represented as an ordered pair as follows: (New York temperature, Orlando temperature).

The teacher can then ask students how they might now represent this graphically. What will the axes be now? An interesting part of the discussion might involve which axis should include the New York temperatures, and which should include the Florida temperatures. Ask students to predict what type of graph they will get if they plot the ordered pairs of temperatures. This now leads to the next task, which, in addition to 8.SP.1 and 8.SP.2, also addresses standard 8.SP.3, "Use the equation of a linear model to solve problems in the context of bivariate measurement data, interpreting the slope and intercept" (NGA Center and CCSSO 2010, p. 56). Since students will also be using the equation of a line to represent the data, this task also addresses the functions standards 8.F.4 and 8.F.5 (NGA Center and CCSSO 2010, p. 55).

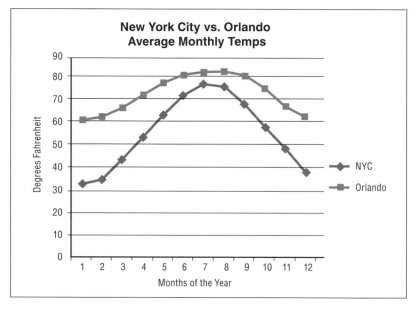

Fig. 4.7. Double line graph comparing average temperatures in New York and Orlando

## Task 4.7

(*a*) Create a scatterplot of the New York City and Orlando average monthly temperatures using New York temperatures for the *x*-values and Orlando temperatures for the *y*-values.

(*b*) Do the points appear to be clustered in any special way? Does there seem to be a positive correlation or a negative correlation? Explain.

(*c*) Take a straightedge and place it where you think it would best approximate the scattering of points that you have plotted. Draw the line on the graph. What could this line help you to do? For example, if you were told it was 58 degrees Fahrenheit in New York City, could you make a good prediction about what the temperature would be in Orlando, Florida? Why or why not? What would your prediction be? Could you have made as good a prediction using the stacked line graphs? Why or why not? Is the line slanted to the right or to the left? What does this mean in terms of the data?

(*d*) Choose two points on the line you made, and use the coordinates of those points to write the equation of your line. What slope did you find? What is its meaning in terms of the context of the problem? What is the *y*-intercept that you found? What is its meaning in terms of the context of the problem?

When examining the scatterplot of the average temperatures in New York and Orlando, students will undoubtedly note a positive correlation. That is, as the average temperature in New York rises, so does the average temperature in Florida. Our scatterplot is in figure 4.8.

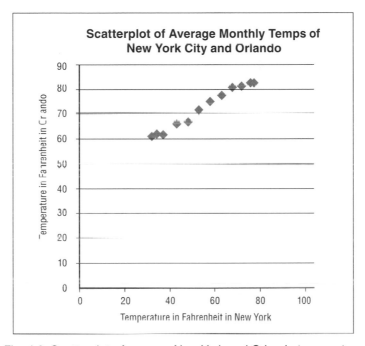

Fig. 4.8. Scatterplot of average New York and Orlando temperatures

Teachers should lead some discussion about the power and limitations of the linear model that students found. Students should be able to explain that the *y*-intercept represents the point where it is 0 degrees Fahrenheit in New York and the corresponding temperature in Orlando is about 50 degrees (depending on the linear model), and that the slope represents the number of degrees that the temperature in Orlando changes based on a change of 1 degree in New York (if slope is expressed as a decimal). So that students do not get the idea that scatterplots always look like ones where there is a positive correlation, students should repeat some modifications of task 4.7 to have them consider other data that might produce scatterplots with different correlations. For example, students can produce a scatterplot like the one in figure 4.9, which shows the negative correlation of average temperatures in New York versus those in Australia. The scatterplot in figure 4.10 shows that there is no apparent linear relationship between the average temperatures in New York versus those in Venezuela.

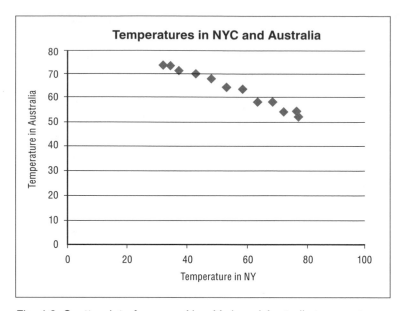

Fig. 4.9. Scatterplot of average New York and Australia temperatures

*Source:* http://www.weatherbase.com/weather/state.php3?c=AU&s=&refer=&countryname=Australia

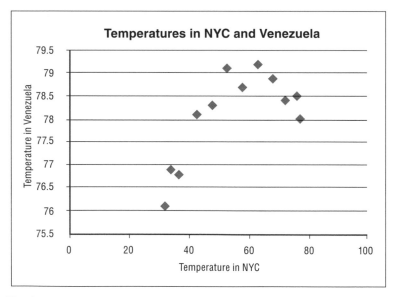

Fig. 4.10. Scatterplot of average New York and Venezuela temperatures

*Source:* http://www.weatherbase.com/weather/city.php3?c=VE&refer=&name=Venezuel

Students can consider questions similar to the ones in task 4.7 but ask whether the values increase or decrease from left to right, or whether there is not much of a linear pattern. Students can also be asked why they think a particular correlation is negative, or why there is not much of a correlation. To get practice creating scatterplots and finding lines of best fit, students might also consult the website http://staff.argyll.epsb.ca/jreed/math9/strand4/scatterPlot.htm. It has an interactive scatterplot maker.

Up to this point, the students have been examining data sets where the variable on each axis is the same, in this case average temperature. They have seen how helpful it can be to examine how the temperatures of two different places are related using one scatterplot. Now the teacher may propose a question such as, "Is the average temperature per month in New York related to the average number of days of precipitation (i.e., rain or snow) each month in New York?" Before embarking on this task, the teacher may want to discuss the measures along each of the axes in the prior problems and suggest different measures that may be compared. Task 4.8 compares the average number of days of precipitation per month to average monthly temperatures in New York. Again, teachers may want to discuss which measure should appear on the *x*-axis and the *y*-axis. As the previous task did, this task addresses standards 8.SP.1, 8.SP.2, and 8.SP.3 and functions standards 8.F.4 and 8.F.5 (NGA Center and CCSSO 2010, pp. 55–56).

## Task 4.8

(*a*) Using a chart, line up the data for the average temperatures per month in New York City and the number of days of precipitation per month in New York City. Do they seem to be related? That is, as the weather gets colder, does the number of days of precipitation increase or decrease?

(*b*) How can you adjust the type of scatterplot you made previously to examine the relationship of temperature and number of days with precipitation? How many variables will you be examining now?

(*c*) Construct a graph with the *x*-axis being average degrees in Fahrenheit and the *y*-axis being number of days of precipitation. Create the coordinates by pairing the data for each month. For example, using the figures in tables 4.4 (p. 63) and 4.6 (p. 70), for January it would be (32, 10), for February it would be (34, 9), and so on. Plot all of the points.

(*d*) Do the points appear to be clustered in any special way? Does there seem to be a positive correlation or a negative correlation? Explain.

(*e*) Based on your response to (*d*) above, what can you say about the relationship between the average temperature per month in New York City and the average number of days of precipitation per month in New York City?

(*f*) Since we are now able to make correlations between bivariate data, look in the newspaper or on the Web for other examples of bivariate data sets that might be of interest to you.

The precipitation data for this task appear in table 4.6. The scatterplot appears in figure 4.11.

Table 4.6

*Average number of days with precipitation in New York, New York*

| Annual | JAN | FEB | MAR | APR | MAY | JUN | JUL | AUG | SEP | OCT | NOV | DEC |
|--------|-----|-----|-----|-----|-----|-----|-----|-----|-----|-----|-----|-----|
| 114 | 10 | 9 | 11 | 11 | 11 | 9 | 8 | 9 | 8 | 7 | 10 | 11 |

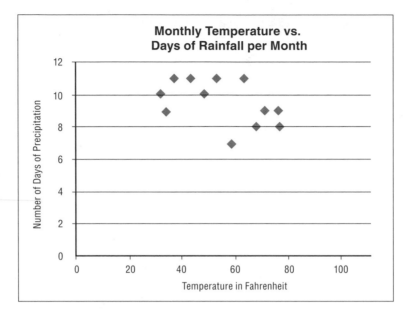

Fig. 4.11. Scatterplot of the number of days of precipitation and average monthly temperature in New York

Students can be encouraged to collect or search for their own data to make their own scatterplots. For example, they can investigate the number of cigarettes smoked per day and the incidence of lung cancer, or they can examine the shoe sizes and heights of their classmates.

## DISCUSSION—*Tasks 4.5 through 4.8*

In each of these tasks concerning the graphing of real data, students have been placed in problem-solving situations in which they must respond to questions that entail a number of different levels of graph comprehension. They must first understand the problem being asked and figure out where they can find the data they need to answer the questions. Once they obtain the data, they must be able to read it and understand the meaning of the numbers they see and the units that are involved. Next, they must figure out the best ways to represent the data and then interpret the graphs that emerge, understanding the scales and the units of measurement. To notice the trends in the data, students must read between the data. Students are also asked to make predictions based on the graphs, requiring them to read "beyond" the data. Such skills not only meet the Common Core Standards but are also essential for students who are confronted with data and graphs on a daily basis.

## MP.1

When examining the disorganized set of data in each of the data sets above, students must be able to make sense of the data and the best ways of relating it and organizing it, thus becoming mathematically proficient students who can "make sense of problems and persevere in solving them" (NGA Center and CCSSO 2010, p. 6).

## MP.2

When graphing the data in each of the problems in this section, students must be able to "contextualize" and "decontextualize," thus "reason[ing] abstractly and quantitatively" (NGA Center and CCSSO 2010, p. 6). In particular, when relating the slope of the line of best fit with the data in the model, students must decontextualize from the original problem in order to compute the slope of the line of best fit, and then contextualize in order to relate the meaning of the slope that was computed in relation to the data in the problem.

## MP.4

In creating the graphs and linear representations of the data presented in the above problems, students are "model[ing] with mathematics," including "identify[ing] important quantities in a practical situation and map[ping] their relationships using such tools as diagrams . . . [and] graphs" (NGA Center and CCSSO 2010, p. 7). Statistical analyses of the problems above lend themselves particularly well to modeling with mathematics.

# Chapter 5

# Expressions, Equations, and Functions

For students in grades 6–8, the Expressions and Equations domain of the Common Core State Standards for Mathematics (CCSSM) provides the framework for linking arithmetic concepts to algebraic expressions, equations, and inequalities. The order of operations and integer exponents are also part of this domain. In addition to setting the foundation for algebra, the standards require that students begin to work informally with functions. In the standards for grade 8, a separate domain for functions only is introduced, one that continues through high school when formal function notation is introduced.

The middle grades are a critical time for working with numerical expressions, understanding expressions involving "letters" (i.e., variables) that stand for numbers, and solving equations and inequalities. There are many misconceptions that present challenges to students who are transitioning from arithmetic to algebraic thinking. Students often have difficulties with abstraction, generalization, and the use of variables. Sometimes these difficulties are grounded in the way students learn arithmetic, which is often as a set of rules and procedures. By middle school, many students see mathematical procedures as arbitrary and disconnected (Ketterlin-Geller et al. 2007), making the transition to algebra difficult.

Equations are a large part of the study of algebra, and an understanding of the notion of equality (and the equal sign) is one of the conceptual underpinnings of solving equations. Misconceptions about the meaning of the equal sign can hinder students' understanding of equations. Students entering the middle grades often see the equal sign as an operator that suggests the "doing" of something, or that "the answer" is coming, instead of as the indicator of an equality relationship (McNeil et al. 2006). For example, students may have difficulty understanding the equation $3 + 4 = 1 + 6$, and they may see this as having a different meaning from $3 + 4 = 7$. This misconception is described as the *operational* view of the equal sign, as opposed to the desirable *relational* view of the equal sign, which describes the equality of two quantities. Further, when evaluating an expression such as $3 + 9 - 7$, many students see no problem with writing $3 + 9 = 12 - 7 = 5$. This reveals a fundamental misunderstanding of equality that will hinder algebraic thinking.

In grade 6, the Expressions and Equations standards are partitioned into three clusters: "Apply and extend previous understandings of arithmetic to algebraic expressions"; "Reason about and solve one-variable equations and inequalities"; and "Represent and analyze quantitative relationships between dependent and independent variables" (National Governors Association Center for Best Practices [NGA Center] and Council of Chief State School Officers [CCSSO] 2010, p. 43–44). The grade 7 standards include two clusters: "Use properties of operations to generate equivalent expressions"; and "Solve real-life and mathematical problems using numerical and algebraic expressions and equations"

(NGA Center and CCSSO 2010, p. 49). The three clusters for grade 8 are "Work with radicals and integer exponents"; "Understand the connections between proportional relationships, lines, and linear equations"; and "Analyze and solve linear equations and pairs of simultaneous linear equations" (NGA Center and CCSSO 2010, p. 54). When students begin to work more formally with functions in grade 8, the new Functions domain includes standards in two clusters: "Define, evaluate, and compare functions" and "Use functions to model relationships between quantities" (NGA Center and CCSSO 2010, p. 55).

The nine tasks in this chapter support evaluating expressions (tasks 5.1, 5.2, 5.3 and 5.4), equations and inequalities (tasks 5.5 and 5.6), simultaneous equations (task 5.7) and functions (tasks 5.8 and 5.9). The eight Standards for Mathematical Practice (MP) listed on page vi are woven throughout these tasks, and, depending on the problem, a relevant subset of those standards is discussed. The problems are loosely grouped by grade level, although the extensions of some problems might allow students to meet a higher grade's standards. As in other chapters, we believe that all of the problems require "attention to precision," thus developing mathematically proficient students as required by the sixth Standard for Mathematical Practice. The tasks in this chapter are summarized in table 5.1.

Table 5.1
*Content areas, grade levels, and standards met by the tasks in chapter 5*

| Content Areas | Task | Grade 6 | Grade 7 | Grade 8 | Mathematical Practice |
|---|---|---|---|---|---|
| Evaluating expressions—Exponents | 5.1 | 6.EE.1 | | | MP.3, MP.7 |
| Evaluating expressions—Order of operations | 5.2 | 6.EE.2c, 6.EE.3, 6.EE.4 | 7.EE.1* | | MP.3 |
| Evaluation expressions—Equality (Functions*) | 5.3 | | 7.EE.2 | 8.F.4, 8.F.5 | MP.4, MP.7 |
| Evaluating expressions—Negative exponents | 5.4 | | | 8.EE.1 | MP.3, MP.7 |
| Equations—Introduction | 5.5 | 6.EE.2a, b, c; 6.EE.5, 6.EE.6 | 7.EE.1* | | MP.1, MP.2 |
| Inequalities | 5.6 | 6.EE.8 | 7.EE.4b* | | MP.1, MP.2, MP.4 |
| Simultaneous equations | 5.7 | | | 8.EE.8 | MP.1, MP. 2, MP.4 |
| Functions | 5.8 | | | 8.F.1, 8.F.3, 8.F.4 | MP.2, MP.4 |
| Functions | 5.9 | | | 8.EE.5, 8.F.4, 8.EE.6* | MP.2, MP.4, MP.8 |

*Extension of the task

**74**

# Evaluating Expressions

## Grades 6 and 7

Task 5.1 is intended to help students develop an understanding of whole number exponents, addressing standard 6.EE.1 on that topic (NGA Center and CCSSO 2010, p. 43). This task is designed to target a common misconception that many students have when working with variables. Teachers may want to let students see part (*b*) only after they have worked on part (*a*). The problem presented here is well suited as a launch for a lesson on whole number exponents.

## Task 5.1

    (*a*) Usha and Josh are working on a problem that involves finding the volume of a cube whose edge measures 5 centimeters. Josh said, "I can do that. You multiply 5 • 3, so the volume is 15 cubic centimeters." Usha is not sure that Josh is correct, because her answer was 125 cubic centimeters. Who is correct? How did Usha compute her answer?

    (*b*) Explain why $6^2$ and 6 • 2 are different. Evaluate each expression. Then explain why $x^5$ and $x$ • 5 are different.

The purpose of task 5.1 is to explore the common misconception that many students have, which is that an exponent has the same meaning as a coefficient. Teachers may want to use a visual aid or a manipulative to relate the meaning of volume to the meaning of raising a number to an exponent of 3. Teachers might also decide to modify the problem to involve area instead of volume, because it is easier to draw a two-dimensional representation of the situation. If the problem is changed to be about area, the given information would involve the side of a square of length 5 centimeters, and Josh's misconception would be to multiply 5 • 2. Usha's answer would then be 25 square centimeters.

    The order of operations is often a source of confusion and misconceptions for students. For several reasons, two commonly used acronyms—*PEMDAS* ("Parentheses, Exponents, Multiplication, Division, Addition, Subtraction") and *BEDMAS* (with *B* standing for "Brackets")—often mislead students and lead to mistakes. We recommend that teachers avoid using this acronym, and that several points are discussed with students when evaluating expressions that involve many operations, exponents, and symbols. Rather than discussing that "parentheses" must be evaluated first, it is a good idea to emphasize that "grouping symbols" should be evaluated first. Of course, grouping symbols include parentheses and brackets, but also include absolute value bars, the radical, and the vinculum (i.e., the fraction bar).

Students often erroneously believe that multiplication must precede division, and that addition must precede subtraction. The conceptual underpinnings of why multiplication and division are done in order from left to right, and why addition and subtraction are done in order from left to right, may not be evident to students until they grasp the concept that division is equivalent to multiplication of the reciprocal of a number (e.g., its multiplicative inverse), and that subtraction is equivalent to addition of the negation of a number (e.g., its additive inverse).

The task that follows gives students an expression and an answer that is possibly incorrect, and it asks them to determine the nature of the mistake made by a fictional student, or determine that the answer is correct. This task gives students the opportunity to critically analyze another "student's" work. In parts (*a*) through (*e*), task 5.2 addresses standard 6.EE.2c, "Perform arithmetic operations, including those involving whole-number exponents, in the conventional order." Parts (*f*) and (*g*) target standard 6.EE.3, "Apply the properties of operations to generate equivalent expressions," and 6.EE.4, "Identify when two expressions are equivalent" (NGA Center and CCSSO 2010, p. 44).

## Task 5.2

For each of the following, a student has evaluated the given expression. Your job is to determine whether the student is correct or not. If you think the student is wrong, explain the mistake and provide the correct answer.

(*a*)  Fiona says that $12 \div 4 \cdot 3 = 1$.

(*b*)  Malia says that $10 - 2(5 + 11) = -22$.

(*c*)  Kevin says that $3 - 2 + 1 - 4 = -2$.

(*d*)  Tyler says that $5^2 + 1^2 = 36$.

(*e*)  Carlos says that $\dfrac{10 + 1 + 4}{5} = 7$

(*f*)  Jennifer says that $2x + 3 = 5x$.

(*g*)  Lillian says that $3(x + 2y) = 3x + 2y$.

Of course, (*b*) and (*c*) are correct, while (*a*) should be 9, (*d*) should be 26, (*e*) should be 3, (*f*) cannot be simplified, and (*g*) should be $3x + 6y$. Fiona, the fictional student in part (*a*), thought that multiplication precedes division, and Tyler, in part (*d*), thought that addition should precede exponents. Carlos divided 10 by 5 before adding $10 + 1 + 4$ in part (*e*); $10 + 1 + 4$ should instead be added first because the vinculum (i.e., the division bar) is a grouping symbol. Jennifer, in part (*f*), does not understand like terms, and Lillian does not understand the distributive property in part (*g*).

Teachers may modify the parts of the task to suit their students' needs, and they can make the problems more or less difficult as appropriate. For example, in part (*b*) teachers

Expressions, Equations, and Functions

may wish to avoid multiplication by a negative number, so the problem could be modified to 10 + 2(5 + 11), which is 42. If a student makes the common mistake of adding 10 + 2 first, the result would be 192. Many other modifications to the above tasks are possible; for example, teachers could involve more advanced grouping symbols, such as the absolute value bars. Teachers may also modify parts (*f*) and (*g*) to involve rational coefficients and thereby meet standard 7.EE.1, "Apply properties of operations as strategies to add, subtract, factor, and expand linear expressions with rational coefficients" (NGA Center and CCSSO 2010, p. 49).

# Grades 7 and 8

Task 5.3 is designed to address standard 7.EE.2, "Understand that rewriting an expression in different forms in a problem context can shed light on the problem and how the quantities in it are related" (NGA Center and CCSSO 2010, p. 49). Students are given contexts in which a percent is either added to or subtracted from a quantity, and examining the general situation can help students see the solution in a different way, which might help them approach problems in the future more easily. It may be helpful for students to set up a recording chart to keep track of their work. The following three headings would be suitable for part (*a*): *Sales this week, Amount added,* and *Sales next week.* For part (*b*) the three headings may be: *Price, Amount deducted,* and *Sale price.*

## Task 5.3

(*a*) Judy sells clothes in a local store. This week, she sold *D* dollars worth of clothes. Her manager tells her that next week she will need to increase her sales by 20 percent.

(1) If $D = 100$, what amount must she sell next week?

(2) If $D = 525$, what amount must she sell next week?

(3) If we don't know how many dollars (*D*) worth of clothes she sold this week, how can we represent how much she must sell the next week?

(*b*) Waleed sees that a store is having a sale for 25 percent off of the price of all of the items in an art supply store. He buys an item that costs *A* dollars.

(1) If $A = 60$, what is the sale price?

(2) If $A = 20$, what is the sale price?

(3) If we don't know the value of *A*, how can we represent the sale price?

Although this problem may seem like a "typical" percent problem, its intent (and the rationale for using a variable to represent the initial amount) is to allow students to see that there is a more efficient way to view the situation, and that the percents added or subtracted do not need to be considered in two parts. In part (*a*), students will likely compute the 20 percent increase for each of the first two amounts, and then add. The third question in part (*a*) requires students to approach the problem a bit differently, and more efficiently. They must consider that for any amount $D$, that $0.2 \cdot D$ is being added to find out the next week's expected sales. If they represent this by $D + 0.2 \cdot D$, considering like terms (or the distributive property) can allow students to see that this is equivalent to $1.2 \cdot D$, or simply $1.2D$. This representation is particularly useful in the future when doing exponential growth problems. Similarly, if students represent the sale price in part (*b*) as $A - 0.25 \cdot A$, like terms or the distributive property lead them to conclude that this is equivalent to $0.75 \cdot A$, or simply $0.75A$. This representation is very practical, since it represents what is actually paid by Waleed in the problem, and more generally by a consumer paying a sale price. It makes much more sense to consider that if there is a "25 percent off" sale then we are paying 75 percent of the original price. This also can help students determine percents "off" mentally, as there is really one fewer step in the calculation.

Further, the relationships in this problem can be considered as functions, thus meeting standard 8.F.4, "Construct a function to model a linear relationship between two quantities," and 8.F.5, "Describe qualitatively the functional relationship between two quantities by analyzing a graph" (NGA Center and CCSS0 2010, p. 55). Students could be asked to write a linear function for part (*a*) and part (*b*). For part (*a*), the amount to be sold for the following week is a function of the sales during the current week. The slope is 1.2, which means that for each dollar sold this week, 1.2 dollars must be sold the following week. For part (*b*), the cost of the item on sale is a function of the original cost. The slope is 0.75, which means that for every dollar increase in original cost, the discounted cost increases by 75 cents.

# Grade 8

Students in grade 8 begin to work with integer exponents, extending their understanding of positive integral exponents to all integral exponents. The following task is intended to help students make sense of the meaning of negative and zero exponents using patterns, addressing the standard 8.EE.1, "know and apply the properties of integer exponents to generate equivalent numerical expressions" (NGA Center and CCSS0 2010, p. 54).

## Task 5.4

Complete the second rows of tables (*a*) through (*c*) using any pattern you notice.

(*a*)

| $2^3$ | $2^2$ | $2^1$ | $2^0$ | $2^{-1}$ | $2^{-2}$ | $2^{-3}$ | $2^{-4}$ |
|-------|-------|-------|-------|----------|----------|----------|----------|
| 8 | 4 | 2 | | | | | |

(b)

| $3^3$ | $3^2$ | $3^1$ | $3^0$ | $3^{-1}$ | $3^{-2}$ | $3^{-3}$ | $3^{-4}$ |
|---|---|---|---|---|---|---|---|
| 27 | 9 | 3 | | | | | |

(c)

| $4^3$ | $4^2$ | $4^1$ | $4^0$ | $4^{-1}$ | $4^{-2}$ | $4^{-3}$ | $4^{-4}$ |
|---|---|---|---|---|---|---|---|
| 64 | 16 | 4 | | | | | |

(d) Examine the entries in the tables. Make a conjecture about what you think raising a number to the exponent zero means, and what raising a number to a negative exponent means. Be sure that you can explain your conjecture.

(e) What is another way to write $12^0$? $5^{-1}$? $x^{-3}$? $(3a)^{-2}$? $3a^{-2}$? $12x^0$? Explain for each.

The tables are designed to allow students to see that each entry in the lower row of the table is obtained by dividing the entry preceding it by the base. In part (a) each subsequent entry is obtained by dividing the one before it by 2; in part (b) each subsequent entry is obtained by dividing the one before it by 3, and in part (c), dividing by 4. Examining the patterns in the tables allows students to make conjectures about the meaning of negative and zero exponents. If teachers wish, they can create several tables similar to the ones in parts (a), (b), and (c) with different bases, have students complete their tables in cooperative groups, and allow groups to compare their tables. For example, for a class with six groups, a teacher could give (a) to group 1, (b) to group 2, and create four additional tables using exponents with different bases. In order to differentiate instruction, teachers may give a group a more challenging table, such as one with a negative base, or use a variable with a coefficient as the base.

## DISCUSSION—*Tasks 5.1 through 5.4*

Each of the above tasks gives students the opportunity to examine the meaning of exponents in different ways. Task 5.1 addresses a common misconception that many students have when learning about exponents, which is that an exponent has the same purpose as a coefficient. When examining the meaning of the exponent using the context of volume, students can see that simply multiplying 5 • 3 does not make sense, especially if they use a concrete model or a drawing to represent the volume. Task 5.2 requires that students examine the work of other fictional students and be able to discuss whether the answer is correct, and if not, what the mistake is. In examining common errors, students may be less likely to make the same errors themselves. Task 5.4 requires that students examine patterns to make a generalization about the meaning of negative exponents and zero exponents.

## MP.3

In task 5.1, students must compare the work of two students to determine which student is using the correct approach using exponents, and be able to explain their thinking. In task 5.2, students must find the mistake made by a fictional student, correct the mistake, and be able to explain both the mistake and the correct answer. By doing this, students are "construct[ing] viable arguments and critiqu[ing] the reasoning of others" (NGA Center and CCSSO 2010, p. 6). Task 5.4 gives students the opportunity to make a conjecture about negative exponents that they must be able to explain and defend.

## MP.4

Task 5.3 provides students with two real-life situations that they are asked to model using an expression, and, if their teacher wishes, as a function. If a function is graphed, students can see the meaning of the slope of each of the lines in the context of the problems.

## MP.7

In comparing the meaning of volume to the evaluation of the expression that represents the volume of the cube in task 5.1, students are "look[ing] for and mak[ing] use of structure" (NGA Center and CCSSO 2010, p. 8). When examining a cube whose edge is 5 centimeters using a concrete model, it should become evident to students that saying that the volume is 15 cubic centimeters is not a sensible answer, especially when examining the "layers" that comprise the cube, and that 5 layers of 25 is equivalent to $5 \cdot 5 \cdot 5$, rather than $5 \cdot 3$. In task 5.3, students are using the structure of the terms in the expression (or function) to view the numerical quantities in the problem in a different way. Similarly, in task 5.4, students are examining the structure of the entries in the table to determine that each is calculated by dividing the prior entry by the base, and they are making a conjecture about the meaning of the negative exponent based upon the patterns they have noticed.

# Equations

## Grades 6 and 7

Students often have trouble with the notion of equality. They may see the equal sign as an "operator" and have difficulty with the idea that two equal expressions can form an equation. Task 5.5 is designed to develop the concept of equations by giving students experience with creating equivalent expressions beginning with the same "secret" number of their choice, and then sharing these equivalent expressions with their peers to determine the value of the secret number. This task helps students meet all parts of standard 6.EE.2, "Write, read and evaluate expressions in which letters stand for numbers" (NGA Center and CCSSO 2010, p. 43). The notion of "variable" is introduced informally in part (*d*); and parts (*d*) and (*e*) begin to address standard 6.EE.5, "Understand solving an equation or inequality as a process of answering a question" and 6.EE.6, "Use variables to represent numbers and write expressions when solving a real-world or mathematical problem" (NGA Center and CCSSO 2010, p. 44). Each of the problems in this section may be used as a launch or a motivational problem for a lesson.

## Task 5.5

(*a*)  Pick a number between 1 and 10. This is your "secret" number.

(*b*)  Using your secret number together with any other numbers you wish, write an expression that "changes" your secret number into the number 25. You may use any arithmetic operations you wish. For example, if your number is 1, your expression may be 1 + 24 or 1 + 3 • 8. There are many ways to do this.

(*c*)  Write four more expressions that change your secret number into 25. Use different operations, symbols, and numbers, including parentheses, exponents, fractions or decimals, and negative numbers. You should have a list of five expressions that change your number into 25. Choose two of your expressions to write equality statements (called *equations*). For example, if two of your expressions are 1 + 24 and 12 • 1 + 13, your equation would be 1 + 24 = 12 • 1 + 13.

(*d*)  Next, get ready to exchange your equations that contain your equivalent expressions with a classmate, who will try to guess your secret number from the equation. Because you don't want anyone to see what your number is, you should use a placeholder for your number. You can use a letter to represent your number. For example, if your secret number is 1 and your expression is 1 + 24, you can use a letter like "n" to stand for your number, so your expression would be *n* + 24 and, as your secret number added to 24 results in 25, your equation could be *n* + 24 = 25 or even *n* + 24 = 12 • *n* + 13.

(*e*)  Exchange your equation with a partner. See whether you can guess your friend's secret number, and if she or he can guess yours. What do you need to do to figure it out? Write down your steps.

The intent of task 5.5 above is to have students see that there are many ways to have a "secret" number (that is, a variable) "change into" another value. Expressions do not need to appear the same to be equal. Students can then informally try to figure out each other's secret number, and teachers can bring in the proper mathematical vocabulary of *variable*. In parts (*d*) and (*e*), teachers may have their students solve each other's equations, rather than working with their expressions; again, the solution should be found using informal reasoning, not formal steps for solving equations. A numerical "pan balance" is available at the link http://illuminations.nctm.org/ActivityDetail.aspx?id=26 so that students can represent their equivalent expressions using numbers. The expressions with variables can be represented at the link http://illuminations.nctm.org/ActivityDetail.aspx?ID=10, where students would indicate their "secret number" as $x$, making sure their scales are balanced.

There are many possible modifications to this problem. If teachers want students to use a broader range of numbers in part (*a*), they can ask their students to choose any number, and not just one from 1 to 10. To make the problem even more challenging, and to practice working with integers, teachers can have the students choose a negative number. Students could also be restricted to negative numbers between –10 and –1. Similarly, in part (*b*), teachers may require that students use fractions to modify the number they chose in part (*a*), which would then allow the problem to address standard 7.EE.1.

The intent of the next exercise, task 5.6, is to target difficulties and conceptual misconceptions that students may have working with a number line to represent the solution set of an inequality. Students have probably been working with continuity models, such as number lines, since elementary grades. However, difficulties with the "continuous" nature of the number line often linger into the middle school grades, based on "discrete" models of number often used in the earlier grades, such as "1 apple, 2 apples," and so on. Technology offers a helpful way to examine the density of the rational and real numbers, such as online number lines that allow students to "zoom" in to view smaller and smaller increments. Similar applications are available on some tablet devices. Task 5.6 targets standard 6.EE.8, "Write an inequality of the form $x > c$ or $x < c$ to represent a constraint or condition in a real-world or mathematical problem" (NGA Center and CCSSO 2010, p. 44).

## Task 5.6

(*a*) Max has a new job in the post office. He has to check and set aside all packages that weigh less than 20 pounds since there is a surcharge on packages that weigh 20 pounds or more. What are some of the possible weights of the packages that weigh less than 20 pounds? Make a list of as many numbers as you can.

(*b*) Have you represented every possible amount on your list? How do you know?

(*c*) Next, create a number line, and plot the numbers you listed on the line. Write down two things you notice.

(*d*) Write an inequality statement to represent the situation.

(*e*) Now, think about how to represent *every* number that is less than 20. How can you do this?

Teachers should initially allow students to work on parts (*a*) through (*c*) of task 5.6 with a minimal amount of guidance, because the nature of the task should reveal students' misconceptions about inequalities, and the notion of "less than." For example, it is likely that initially, students will list only integers less than 20. Teachers may then prompt students to think more broadly about non-integral amounts, at which point students may list familiar fractions, such as 1.5, 2.5, and so on. Teachers should elicit that all values less than 20 (and in this case greater than 0) must be represented. When representing the solution using a number line, curiously, students often "skip" the values between 19 and 20, beginning their solution at the number 19. Teachers can question their students about why they did this. The last part of the problem has students remove the context of the situation and consider *all* values less than 20. In this case, the solution would be extended in the negative direction infinitely. It is interesting to consider that the solution to both the question in context and in the abstract is infinite, although the solution set "seems" larger in the abstract. Of course, teachers may modify the context of the problem to suit the interests of their students; the direction of the inequality may also be changed.

In order to address standard 7.EE.4b, "Solve word problems leading to inequalities of the form $px + q > r$ or $px + q < r$, where $p$, $q$, and $r$ are specific rational numbers" (NGA Center and CCSSO 2010, p. 49), the problem may be modified to require an inequality with a two-step solution. For example, a modification might be as follows:

> Lanette has $10 to spend on groceries. She needs a loaf of bread that costs $2.50. She also wants to buy as much cheese as possible. Cheese is $1.65 per pound. What is the largest amount of cheese she can buy?

Teachers may think of many other modifications to suit their students' needs and interests.

# Grade 8

In grade 8, students begin to work with simultaneous linear equations. Task 5.7 gives students a semiconcrete experience with solving simultaneous equations (also called *systems of equations*). In this task, shapes are being used informally as variables in a problem that can be presented to students as a puzzle. This problem sets the conceptual foundation for standard 8.EE.8b, "Solve systems of two linear equations in two variables algebraically" (NGA Center and CCSSO 2010, p. 55).

## Task 5.7

If ♥ + ♥ + ♥ + ★ + ★ = 18

And ♥ + ★ = 8

What is the value of one ♥ ? What is the value of one ★ ?

Because of its visual nature, the problem may seem a bit simplistic at first, but the reasoning required to determine the value of one "heart" and one "star" is analogous to the reasoning required to solve a system of equations. One approach to use may be that if one heart and one star is 8, then two hearts and two stars is 16. Comparing this to the top equation would make one heart equal to 2, and since one heart and one star equals 8, then one star equals 6. We consider the analogous system of equations:

$$3x + 2y = 18$$
$$x + y = 8.$$

Similar to the pictorial example above, an approach to solving this system would be to multiply the bottom equation by 2, subtract it from the other equation to determine that $x$ is 2, and then substitute into $x + y = 8$ to determine that $y = 6$.

Teachers may also decide to provide a context for the variables. A possible context for the problem above might be the following:

> Boxes of vanilla cupcakes come in one size, and boxes of chocolate cupcakes come in another. Each box of vanilla cupcakes holds $V$ cupcakes, while each box of chocolate cupcakes holds $C$ cupcakes. If three boxes of vanilla cupcakes and two boxes of chocolate cupcakes contain a total of 18 cupcakes, while one box of vanilla cupcakes and one box of chocolate cupcakes contain a total of 8 cupcakes, how many vanilla cupcakes are in each box? How many chocolate cupcakes are in each box?

Finally, students can be asked to make a table of values for each of the equations and graph them on the same set of axes, in order to see that the lines will intersect at the ordered pair (2, 6), thus meeting standard 8.EE.8c, "Solve real-world and mathematical problems leading to two linear equations in two variables." Requiring students to find a graphical solution meets standard 8.EE.8a, "Understand that solutions to a system of two linear equations in two variables correspond to points of intersection of their graphs" (NGA Center and CCSSO 2010, p. 55).

## DISCUSSION—*Tasks 5.5 through 5.7*

Tasks 5.5, 5.6, and 5.7 each give students the opportunity to apply problem-solving techniques to unfamiliar situations. Each problem might require students to take a "different point of view" and examine them from perspectives that might not initially be obvious.

### MP.1

In solving the unfamiliar problems presented in each of the above tasks, students must "make sense of problems and persevere in solving them" (NGA Center and CCSSO 2010, p. 6). Task 5.5 asks students to consider different ways to represent a particular number using a number they have selected themselves. They must determine ways to figure out their partner's "secret" number using an approach of their choosing. Task 5.7 gives a pictorial representation of a system of linear equations that they must make sense of and persevere in solving.

## MP.2

Each of the above tasks provides students with the opportunity to "reason abstractly and quantitatively" (NGA Center and CCSSO 2010, p. 6). Tasks 5.5 and 5.6 ask students to "make sense of quantities and their relationships": In task 5.5, this is done in order to write equivalent expressions, and in task 5.6 it is done in order to relate the representation of the solution set to the number line. Students must "contextualize" and "decontextualize" the quantities in both tasks 5.5 and 5.6. In task 5.6, students must relate the number line to the solution set in the context of the problem, and then to the abstract situation in which "all" numbers less than 20 must be represented. Task 5.6 gives several different contexts for the same problem: pictorial, graphic, algebraic, and in the form of a real-life situation. Students must fluently move between these representations, "attending to the meaning of quantities" (NGA Center and CCSSO 2010, p.6).

## MP.4

The problem in task 5.6 gives students a real-life situation that they must "model with mathematics" (NGA Center and CCSSO 2010, p. 7). They must determine a mathematical representation for the real-life situation in the problem. The real-life context in task 5.7 also gives students the opportunity to model a real-life situation using a system of simultaneous equations.

# Functions

## Grade 8

*Principles and Standards for School Mathematics* (NCTM 2000) stresses the value of incorporating the notion of *function* into the middle school curriculum, and it states that students should work with patterns, relations, and functions, with a focus on linear functions. Among the big ideas behind functions are that they are rules that uniquely assign sets of numbers, and that they can be represented through a variety of modes of representation, including graphs, tables, and verbal descriptions (Van de Walle 1998).

Task 5.8 provides an introduction to functions through a growing pattern. Students can generalize the pattern verbally or using variables. This task addresses the standards 8.F.1, "Understand that a function is a rule that assigns to each input exactly one output. The graph of a function is the set of ordered pairs consisting of an input and the corresponding output"; 8.F.3, "Interpret the equation $y = mx + b$ as defining a linear function"; and 8.F.4, "Construct a function to model a linear relationship between two quantities" (NGA Center and CCSSO 2010, p. 55).

## Task 5.8

Maya made a pattern of drawings. The drawings looked like figure 5.1.

| Drawing 1 | Drawing 2 | Drawing 3 | Drawing 4 |
|-----------|-----------|-----------|-----------|
| X | X | X | X |
| XXX | XXX | XXX | XXX |
| | XXX | XXX | XXX |
| | | XXX | XXX |
| | | | XXX |

Fig. 5.1. Pattern drawings

(*a*) What is the next drawing in the pattern?

(*b*) What is the tenth drawing in the pattern? What is the 100th? Can you draw it? Can you describe it in words?

(*c*) What is the *n*th drawing in the pattern? Describe how you know.

(*d*) Form 5 ordered pairs to represent the five drawings. For example, the first ordered pair would be (1, 4), where 1 represents the pattern number and 4 represents the number of elements in the pattern. Use the first five drawings to make your ordered pairs.

(*e*) Plot the ordered pairs on a coordinate grid. Is there any relationship between each of the points you plotted? Could you predict what the next few points would be? Plot those next points.

(*f*) Now connect the points to form a line. What is the slope of the line? What is the *y*-intercept? Do the slope and *y*-intercept relate to the drawings? Does the line accurately represent the progression of drawings? Explain.

For this task, the generalized pattern would be that the *n*th drawing is represented by $3n + 1$; verbally, students might say that "it is one more than three times the drawing number." There are some important points that teachers may want to discuss in implementing this problem. An important distinction should be made between the ordered pairs that represent the progression of drawings and the line connecting those ordered pairs. Since the function based on the drawing can only take on integral values, the line is not an accurate representation of the situation. It is interesting to see that the slope of the line is the same as the number of *X*s in each row, and that the *y*-intercept is the single *X* that would be in drawing 0, but it is important to emphasize that only positive integral values of *n* relate back to the drawing. For example, the point (–1, –2) is on the line, but it is meaningless in the context of the drawings. The drawings provide a visual representation for students to see that for each subsequent drawing *y* increases by 3, and that this is the slope of the line representing the function when graphed, but also that the "line"

has a restricted domain of non-negative integers. Teachers may want to give part (*f*) only after parts (*a*) through (*e*) are completed.

Several possible modifications and extensions of the problem can be made. Teachers may ask students to create their own patterns, with either a greater or lesser rate of change. For example, if a student wanted to create a pattern with an associated function with a greater rate of change, she or he might change the above pattern to one with rows of four (or more). Another possible modification would be to give a function and then ask students to create a series of drawings that would be represented by the function. For example, if a teacher wanted students to create a pattern based on $y = 5x + 2$, students may have a pattern of drawings with rows of 5 and 2 on top, or one of many other possibilities.

The next task builds a function from a proportional relationship. This type of relationship is sometimes called *direct variation*. This task targets standards 8.EE.5, "Graph proportional relationships, interpreting the unit rate as the slope of the graph" (NGA Center and CCSSO 2010, p. 54) and, as task 5.8 did, standard 8.F.4.

## Task 5.9

Rachel is cooking some food for a party. She wants to make sure that she has enough food for all of her guests, but she is not sure how many guests she is having. She plans on making one cup of rice for every four people.

(*a*) Complete table 5.3 for the amount of rice for each number of guests.

Table 5.2
*Amount of rice for each number of guests*

| Number of guests | 4 | 8 | 12 | 16 | $x$ |
|---|---|---|---|---|---|
| Amount of rice (in cups) | 1 | 2 | | | |

(*b*) Consider each pair of numbers above as an ordered pair, with the top number first. Plot each ordered pair on the coordinate plane. Connect the points. What type of graph did you obtain?

(*c*) Find the slope of the line you graphed in part (*b*). How does the slope relate to the amount of rice needed? Explain the slope in the context of the problem.

(*d*) Is the line you graphed in part (*b*) an accurate representation of this problem? Before answering, consider the question of whether $x$ can take all values in the line. Using this linear model, in terms of the context of this problem, what does *slope* mean?

Depending on the direction the teacher wishes to take, several modifications to this problem would meet different standards. In order to meet standard 8.EE.6, "Use similar triangles to explain why the slope *m* is the same between any two distinct points on a non-vertical line in the coordinate plane" (NGA Center and CCSSO 2010, p. 54), teachers could form pairs of similar triangles using the line graphed. The ratio of corresponding sides of any pair of similar triangles formed by the line, the *x*-axis, and an altitude should be equal, and it should be equal to the slope. This can help shed light on why slope is the same between any two points on a given line (see fig. 5.2).

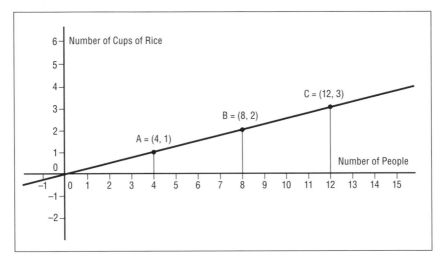

Fig. 5.2. Slopes are the same between any two points on the same line.

In order to meet the second part of standard 8.EE.5, "Compare two different proportional relationships represented in different ways" (NGA Center and CCSSO 2010, p. 54), teachers can give students the graph of a line that represents a different ratio of food to guests at a party and ask them to determine whether there is a greater amount of food represented by this graph than the original. In the extension of the problem, it is important to give different numbers for guests so students will need to examine the graph to determine which is greater. Another possibility for extension would be to have students create a table that has a greater (or lesser) rate of change and to ask them to explain how they know that it is greater (or less).

## DISCUSSION—*Tasks 5.8 and 5.9*

In approaching the above two tasks, students should be formulating plans and attempting different approaches to solving the problems presented. In both tasks, they must make a conceptual leap from considering a relationship numerically to representing a relationship generally as a function, and they will need to explain slope and its meaning in the context of the problem.

## MP.2

Both of these problems require students to "reason abstractly and quantitatively," since in each problem they must flexibly move between the real-life situation and its graphic or tabular representation (NGA Center and CCSSO 2010, p. 6). Students should be able to discuss the meaning of slope in the context of the problem and in the abstract. Students should also be able to determine the greater rate of change by examining the graph and then contextualizing the rate of change to the meaning of the problem.

## MP.4

Since both of the problems in tasks 5.8 and 5.9 represent real-life situations, students are "model[ing] with mathematics" (NGA Center and CCSSO 2010, p. 7). They must determine the graph that represents each situation and explain the meaning of slope in the context of the problem. Most importantly, they must carefully examine the models that they arrive at and determine whether or not there are any limitations caused by representing a concrete problem with an abstract representation such as a graph.

## MP.8

In examining the patterns in task 5.8, and by creating their own patterns and writing functions to represent the patterns, students are "look[ing] for and express[ing] regularity in repeated reasoning" (NGA Center and CCSSO 2010, p. 8). Students need to examine the drawings and determine which aspects of the drawings remain the same, which change, and how they change. They must then determine how to generalize these patterns.

# Appendix

## CCSS Overview for Middle and High School Mathematics

**CONTENT**

| | Ratio and Proportion | The Number System/Number and Quantity | Expressions and Equations/Algebra | Geometry | Statistics and Probability | Functions | Modeling |
|---|---|---|---|---|---|---|---|
| **Grade 6** | • Understand ratio concepts and use ratio reasoning to solve problems. | • Apply and extend previous understandings of multiplication and division to divide fractions by fractions. | • Apply and extend previous understandings of arithmetic to algebraic expressions. | • Solve real-world and mathematical problems involving area, surface area, and volume. | • Develop understanding of statistical variability. | | |
| | | • Compute fluently with multidigit numbers and find common factors and multiples. | • Reason about and solve one-variable equations and inequalities. | | • Summarize and describe distributions. | | |
| | | • Apply and extend previous understandings of numbers to the system of rational numbers. | • Represent and analyze quantitative relationships between dependent and independent variables. | | | | |

## CONTENT

| | Ratio and Proportion | The Number System/Number and Quantity | Expressions and Equations/ Algebra | Geometry | Statistics and Probability | Functions | Modeling |
|---|---|---|---|---|---|---|---|
| **Grade 7** | • Analyze proportional relationships and use them to solve real-world and mathematical problems. | • Apply and extend previous understandings of operations with fractions to add, subtract, multiply, and divide rational numbers. | • Use properties of operations to generate equivalent expressions. | • Draw, construct, and describe geometrical figures and describe the relationships between them. | • Use random sampling to draw inferences about a population. | | |
| | | | • Solve real-life and mathematical problems using numerical and algebraic expressions and equations. | • Solve real-life and mathematical problems involving angle measure, area, surface area, and volume. | • Draw informal comparative inferences about two populations. | | |
| | | | | | • Investigate chance processes and develop, use, and evaluate probability models. | | |

| | The Number System/Number and Quantity | Expressions and Equations/Algebra | Geometry | Statistics and Probability | Functions | Modeling |
|---|---|---|---|---|---|---|
| **Ratio and Proportion** | • Know that there are numbers that are not rational, and approximate them by rational numbers. | • Work with radicals and integer exponents. | • Understand congruence and similarity using physical models, transparencies, or geometry software. | • Investigate patterns of association in bivariate data. | • Define, evaluate, and compare functions. | |
| **Grade 8** | | • Understand the connections between proportional relationships, lines, and linear equations. | • Understand and apply the Pythagorean theorem. | | • Use functions to model relationships between quantities. | |
| | | • Analyze and solve linear equations and pairs of simultaneous linear equations. | • Solve real-world and mathematical problems involving volume of cylinders, cones, and spheres. | | | |

## CONTENT

| | Ratio and Proportion | The Number System/Number and Quantity | Expressions and Equations/Algebra | Geometry | Statistics and Probability | Functions | Modeling |
|---|---|---|---|---|---|---|---|
| **High School** | | • Extend the properties of exponents to rational exponents. | • Interpret the structure of expressions. | • Experiment with transformations in the plane. | • Summarize, represent, and interpret data on a single count or measurement variable. | • Understand the concept of a function and use function notation. | • Model real-world situations across curriculum. |
| | | • Use properties of rational and irrational numbers. | • Write expressions in equivalent forms to solve problems. | • Understand congruence in terms of rigid motions. | • Summarize, represent, and interpret data on two categorical and quantitative variables. | • Interpret functions that arise in applications in terms of the context. | |
| | | • Reason quantitatively and use units to solve problems. | • Perform arithmetic operations on polynomials. | • Prove geometric theorems. | • Interpret linear models. | • Analyze functions using different representations. | |
| | | • Perform arithmetic operations with complex numbers. | • Understand the relationship between zeros and factors of polynomials. | • Make geometric constructions. | • Understand and evaluate random processes underlying statistical experiments. | • Build a function that models a relationship between two quantities. | |
| | | • Represent complex numbers and their operations on the complex plane. | • Use polynomial identities to solve problems. | • Understand similarity in terms of similarity transformations. | • Make inferences and justify conclusions from sample surveys, experiments and observational studies. | • Build new functions from existing functions. | |

# References

Allen, Pamela. *Mr. Archimedes' Bath.* New York: Lothrop, Lee & Shepard Books, 1980.

Curcio, F. R. "Comprehension of Mathematical Relationships Experienced in Graphs." *Journal for Research in Mathematics Education* 18 (November 1987): 382–93.

Fuys, David, Dorothy Geddes, and Rosamond Tischler. "The van Hiele Model of Thinking in Geometry among Adolescents." *Journal for Research in Mathematics Education.* Monograph. Volume 3. Reston, Va.: National Council of Teachers of Mathematics, 1988.

Henderson, Kenneth B., and Robert E. Pingry. "Problem-solving in Mathematics." In *The Learning of Mathematics: Its Theory and* Practice, 1953 Yearbook of the National Council of Teachers of Mathematics (NCTM), edited by Howard F. Fehr, pp. 228–70. Washington, D.C.: NCTM, 1953.

Hendrick, Bill. "Percentage of Overweight, Obese Americans Swells." *WebMD Health News,* http://www.webmd.com/diet/news/20100210/percentage-of-overweight-obese-americans-swells, February 10, 2010.

Ketterlin Geller, Leanne R., Kathleen Jungjohann, David J. Chard, and Scott Baker. "From Arithmetic to Algebra." *Educational Leadership* 65 (November 2007): 66–71.

Lesh, Richard, and Judith Zawojewski. "Problem Solving and Modeling." In *Second Handbook of Research on Mathematics Teaching and Learning,* edited by Frank K. Lester, Jr., pp. 763–804. Charlotte, N.C.: Information Age Publishing, and Reston, Va.: National Council of Teachers of Mathematics, 2007.

Lester, Frank K., and Paul E. Kehle. "From Problem Solving to Modeling: The Evolution of Thinking about Research on Complex Mathematical Activity." In *Beyond Constructivism,* edited by Richard Lesh and Helen M. Doerr, pp. 501–17. Mahwah, N.J.: Lawrence Erlbaum Associates, 2003.

McNeil, Nicole M., Laura Grandau, Eric J. Knuth, Martha W. Alibali, Ana C. Stephens, Shanta Hattikudur, and Daniel E. Krill. "Middle-School Students' Understanding of the Equal Sign: The Books They Read Can't Help." *Cognition and Instruction,* 24 (2006): 367–85.

National Council of Teachers of Mathematics (NCTM). *An Agenda for Action.* Reston, Va.: NCTM, 1980.

———. Essential Understanding Series. Reston, Va.: NCTM, 2010–13.

———. Reasoning and Sense Making Series. Reston, Va.: NCTM, 2010.

———. *Principles and Standards for School Mathematics.* Reston, Va.: NCTM, 2000.

———. *Making It Happen: A Guide to Interpreting and Implementing Common Core State Standards for Mathematics.* Reston, Va.: NCTM, 2011.

National Governors Association Center for Best Practices and Council of Chief State School Officers (NGA Center and CCSSO). *Common Core State Standards for Mathematics.* Washington, D.C.: NGA Center and CCSSO, 2010. http://www.corestandards.org.

O'Daffer, Phares, ed. *Problem Solving: Tips for Teachers.* Reston, Va.: NCTM, 1988.

Pollak, Henry. "Introduction: What Is Mathematical Modeling?" In *Mathematical Modeling Handbook*, edited by Heather Gould, Diane R. Murray, and Andrew Sanfratello, pp. vii–xi. Bedford, Mass.: COMAP, 2011.

Pólya, George. *How to Solve It,* 2nd ed. Princeton, N.J.: Princeton University Press, 1957.

Schoenfeld, Alan H. "Problem Solving in the United States, 1970–2008: Research and Theory, Practice and Politics." *ZDM Mathematics Education* 39 (2007): 537–51.

Schwartz, Sydney L. *Implementing the Common Core State Standards through Mathematical Problem Solving: Kindergarten–Grade 2.* Reston, Va.: National Council of Teachers of Mathematics, 2013.

Shaughnessy, J. Michael, Joan Garfield, and Brian Greer. "Data Handling." In *International Handbook of Mathematics Education,* edited by Alan J. Bishop, Ken Clements, Christine Keitel, Jeremy Kilpatrick, and Colette Laborde. Dordrecht, the Netherlands: Kluwer, 1996, pp. 205–37.

Urich, Joshua A., and Elizabeth A. Sasse. "An Ap'peel'ing Activity." *Mathematics Teaching in the Middle School* 105 (October 2011): 189–93.

Van de Walle, John A. *Elementary and Middle School Mathematics: Teaching Developmentally,* 3rd ed. New York: Longman, 1998.

Watson, Jane M., and Jonathan B. Moritz. "The Longitudinal Development of Understanding of Average." *Mathematical Thinking and Learning* 2 (2000): 11–50.

Wells, H. G. *Mankind in the Making.* New York: Scribner, 1903/2004.